I'm Just A DJ But...

It Makes Sense to Me

I'm Just A DJ But...
It Makes Sense to Me

TOM JOYNER

WITH MARY FLOWERS BOYCE

WARNER BOOKS

New York   Boston

Warner Books

Time Warner Book Group
1271 Avenue of the Americas, New York, NY 10020
Visit our Web site at www.twbookmark.com.

Printed in the United States of America

First Edition: September 2005
10 9 8 7 6 5 4 3 2 1

Library of Congress Cataloging-in-Publication Data
Joyner, Tom.
    I'm just a deejay but— it makes sense to me / Tom
Joyner, with Mary Flowers Boyce.— 1st ed.
        p.   cm.
    ISBN 0-446-57676-X
    1. Joyner, Tom.   2. African American disc jockeys—
Biography.   I. Boyce, Mary Flowers.   II. Title.
    ML429.J83A3   2005
    791.4402'8'092—dc22   2005011916

Dedication

To my crew, Sybil, J, Myra, Jedda, Tavis, and Mary

Acknowledgments

I have a lot of people to thank and I'm lifting my rule of not doing "shout-outs" for this occasion.

Thanks to my sons, Oscar and Thomas, for giving me so much to be proud of.

Thanks to my wife, Donna, for bringing love and joy into my life and loving me enough to hide the snacks.

Thanks to my daddy, H. L. Joyner, for tough love back in the day and sweet love later (much later), and to my mom, Buddy, for showing me nothing but love from the very beginning.

Thanks to my big and much older brother, Albert Joyner, a man who works as hard as I do, my sister-in-law, Danita, and to my nieces and nephew, Allison, Danielle, and Bubba, for keeping me "happenin'."

Thanks to David Kantor, the man who showed me how to make big money in radio by giving me my first shot at a nationally syndicated morning radio show and is the only boss that I could call a friend.

Thanks to all my staff at Reach Media, especially Julia Atherton for her marketing expertise.

Thanks to my coauthor, Mary Flowers Boyce, and editors Irene Prokop and Frances Jalet-Miller.

Special thanks to Denise Stinson of Walk Worthy Press for hooking me up with Warner Books and making this whole project happen.

Thanks to DeWayne Wickham for hooking me up with Denise Stinson.

Thanks to John H. Johnson for teaching me so much about life, business, and to never forget who my audience is.

Thank you to Historically Black Colleges and Universities that continue to educate and nurture African American kids, and finally thanks to the entire town of Tuskegee, Alabama, for teaching me that no dream is out of reach.

Contents

Introduction

I've had a lot of goals in my life but until fairly recently writing a book wasn't one of them. For that matter, in reality I'm not even a big reader, but you wouldn't know it if you walked into my office at home. There's an entire wall of bookshelves and the shelves are filled with books that people have sent to me. Hundreds. They look great, and when people visit they gasp and ask, "Have you really read all of these books?" I usually pretend like I don't hear them and change the subject.

Now this is not to say I don't read books at all. I do love books about real people that tell me about their journeys to success—their challenges, their influences, their mistakes, their victories—that's fascinating to me.

When the opportunity came for me to write a book, I decided to write the kind I would want to read—something that could possibly help inspire someone to believe in his dreams, work hard to achieve them, and give back once he's made it.

More than that, I wanted to write something that would reach people who might be thinking they don't have what it takes to become a success—something to serve as a reminder that ordinary people can do extraordinary things.

Many people are interested in getting rich quick and I can't tell anyone how to do that. But I can tell you about something even better than getting rich quick: It is finding something you love doing and getting paid for doing it. I can't promise that it will make you rich but I do promise you that always working hard to be the best at what you do pays off in the end.

Being a deejay wasn't the only career I attempted, but it is the one I've worked at hardest and longest to succeed. And it has paid off—and not just monetarily. It's given me a chance to fly to South Africa to be part of a delegation led by President Clinton, to be grand marshal at the Zulu Parade in New Orleans for Mardi Gras, and to bring a live broadcast to soldiers and their families in Fort Hood, Texas, during the war in Iraq.

It's also given me the opportunity to talk to millions of mostly African Americans each morning on the *Tom Joyner Morning Show*, and over the years we've talked about everything from the Electric Slide to the electoral college and everybody from Colin Powell to Raven. This book gives me a chance to share a little about what I've learned and observed over the years and why targeting and serving my core audience will always be a priority.

The more I wrote, the more I wanted to recognize and address people and issues who have had an impact on my life—women like my aunts in my past and female members of the *Tom Joyner Morning Show* and Reach Media, Inc. today; my daddy who practiced "tough love" before it was invented and my sons who grew up to become my bosses; racism, black pride, and whether naming your child after an alcoholic beverage hurts her chances in the job market.

There's something for you if you aren't African American, too—an insight into some of the things black folks discuss when we get home from work: what makes us laugh, what make us cringe, and why it's so stressful for us to watch most reality shows.

Once I got into the book, writing began to get good to me. I bought a jacket with patches on the sleeves, a pipe, and an ascot. I'm even thinking of changing my name to F. Scott Tom Joyner—it sounds a lot more literary. Maybe all those honorary degrees I got from Historically Black Colleges and Universities—HBCUs—over the years were starting to make me smarter. Maybe this C-minus student could redeem himself. (See the chapter on dreaming!)

Television shows, movies, and even this book are all ventures that I'm excited to be part of, but at the end of the day I am smart enough not to give up my morning job. I haven't forgotten who I am: just a deejay.

I'm Just A DJ But...

It Makes Sense to Me

chapter one

Get Up Offa That Dream!

*The most successful people
envision themselves doing
more and becoming more.*

'M JUST a deejay but I've always been a big dreamer. Some of my dreams have come true, some haven't; but I believe dreaming big has helped me reach my goals. When I was a little boy growing up in Tuskegee, Alabama, I loved to watch a popular television show called *The Millionaire*. The show's main character was this guy who worked for a multimillionaire and his job each week was to give away to some unsuspecting person a check for $1 million. I never missed an episode, but I would get frustrated because I always thought I could do a better job at distributing that money! For some reason, the recipients of the $1 million would find a way to mess the money up. I would go to bed thinking if I had that $1 million, I would know what to do with it. I was positive that I wouldn't blow it. I'd drift off to sleep with a smile on my face as I dreamed about how I would spend it. I've been dreaming ever since.

The most successful people envision themselves doing more and becoming more, so don't ever let anyone tell you that dreaming (envisioning) is a waste of time. Dreaming allows you to think outside of the box. You have to be able to imagine what things could be like beyond the situation you are currently in. Until you do, you will be more likely to settle for the status quo. There are people who are perfectly fine going along day to day taking whatever life hands them—I'm not one of them.

The town I was raised in was full of big dreamers. In fact, most of the people who came to Tuskegee came there in the first place following a dream to improve their lives. Men like my daddy came there with hopes and dreams of becoming Tuskegee Airmen, which was the first group of black men to fly airplanes for the U.S. military. He didn't make it but he gave it a good try, and he'd tell you all about it if you asked him. But you'd better pull up a chair and get yourself a glass of sweet tea. It's a long story!

Booker T. Washington, the founder of the Tuskegee Institute, had to have been a big dreamer. Here's a man who was born into slavery. When he became president of Tuskegee Institute in 1881, the school barely existed, but thanks to his fund-raising efforts it became one of the leading facilities for educating blacks in the country. When you hear a story like that you just want to walk up to some lazy, whining, black folks and slap them right across the head.

Rosa Parks, who was born in Tuskegee, must have had a dream to be treated with respect by white folks. What some people may not realize is the day she refused to give up her seat on the bus to a white man wasn't the first time she had been treated poorly by white folks. As a child she was threatened and yelled at by parents of white children for trying to protect herself and her little brother from bullies. That was back around 1920. So, by the time 1955 rolled around I'm thinking Ms. Parks was ready to take on the white bus driver and anybody else. That action led to the 381-day Montgomery bus boycott and the civil rights movement was born.

One of my biggest dreams was to become a success in the music industry. During my freshman year at Tuskegee Institute, a group of students including Lionel Richie formed a group that would compete in the freshman talent show. The singers were called the DuPonts and the band that backed us was the Commodores. After the talent show we began getting regular gigs around town. I was the show closer. At first I would fall on my knees and sing. Then I tried to step my act up a little bit, and, instead of just falling on my knees, I'd jump up and fall on my knees. Then I would climb on top of stuff and fall on my knees. By the end I was starting at the back of the stage, taking a running leap and sliding to the front of the stage on my knees. I would let out a loud scream like James Brown, but actually I was screaming out of pain. I tore my knees up along with a lot of cheap pairs of pants. I wasn't the greatest singer but what I lacked in singing I made up in acrobatics.

At some point we got two offers, one from a local marketing guy from New York and one from a flashy New York gangster. The gangster wanted us to move to New York. The local guy from New York thought we should stay in Tuskegee and get our degrees. My family agreed that continuing my education was the best decision, so I quit the group. The DuPonts moved to New York with the gangster guy, got a record deal, put out a couple of records, but never did much of anything, and the gangster guy went to jail. The Commodores, however, remained in Tuskegee with the local guy Benny Ashburn and Benny took them to the top—without me or my bad knees! Seeing those guys become huge R&B successes made me work harder than ever to do something big just so I wouldn't be kicking myself for the rest of my life.

I wasn't an overnight success in radio, but once I made up my mind I was going to make a career of it, I aspired to go to the top. No matter what kind of job or career you have, if you aim high it can pay off big in the end. You're only helping yourself when you try to take it to the top. Even if you only get halfway there, you're better off than you would have been if you hadn't tried at all. When I was trying so hard to make it in radio, I had no idea that so many changes and opportunities would be available to me in the future. Radio syndication, TV syndication, mergers, satellite radio, and who knows what else was down the road. I just knew that if I did really well in the radio business, the next horizon would be television. No matter how well you do in radio, there will be some people out there who think you haven't really made it until you're on TV, and as good as radio has been to me, I have to admit, I thought television was the bomb!

After having a good run in several markets and doing really well at station WJPC in Chicago in the '80s, I retired from radio. John H. Johnson, the publishing mogul and owner of the AM radio station, had promised when he hired me that if I could make his poor-performing station number two in the Chicago market he would put me on television. It was an offer I couldn't refuse. I wasn't sure if I could deliver, but I wanted to be on TV so bad, I gave it all I had. I worked hard doing all kinds of promotions and stunts to get the radio station and my name out there. I brought the ratings way up and Mr. Johnson kept his end of the bargain. The station gave me a huge going-away party and a parade down Michigan Avenue, and the syndicated television show *Ebony/Jet Showcase* was born. I was taking that step from local fame as a radio deejay to national stardom on TV . . . sort of.

As bad as I wanted to have my own TV show, however, I really knew nothing about running a TV show. And hear me when I say, I was *running* it. I was the host, the producer, the director, the tape editor, and I had to sell advertising time for the show too, and it was all new to me. I think I made every mistake possible but mainly I paid way too much money for production. On shoots where it should have been just me and a cameraman, I would show up with a big truck and a gang of people. Steven Spielberg shot entire films with smaller crews.

One day I showed up on the set of the TV series *Fame*, and my crew was bigger than the one *Fame* had. Not only did *I* not know what I was doing, my guests knew it too. Debbie Allen felt so bad for me, she said, "Sit down, child. This is ridiculous. All you need is one cameraman and one soundman!" She pointed out that I was using up most of my budget feeding lunch to all my people!

Aretha Franklin had so much sympathy for me, she cooked for me and the entire crew—fried ribs. Yes, that's what I said. That's why I love her so much to this day. As many times as she's been on the *Tom Joyner Morning Show* she's never said a word about how I made a fool out of myself years earlier.

Even though *Ebony/Jet Showcase* failed after just twenty-six episodes, I learned some invaluable lessons. The main one is this: If you fail at something, take the part that worked and turn it into something else. Admittedly there were some things wrong with *Ebony/Jet Showcase* but there were a lot of right things too, and those are the things I concentrated on. In most failures you can find something positive. And that's what gives you the drive to try again. During my run on *Ebony/Jet* I met and interviewed Sammy Davis Jr., Stevie Wonder, Flip Wilson, and Bill Cosby and I conducted one of the last interviews Michael Jackson would do for a long time. Coincidence? Maybe not. But my point is, doing that show got me accustomed to interviewing big stars and many of the elements of *Ebony/Jet Showcase* are used on the *Tom Joyner Morning Show*.

Another thing I learned is the only way you can get good at something is to just do it. Whether you have a dream to become a performer, a writer, or a cook, just dreaming about it, or even talking about it, will get you nowhere. You have to get out there and try it—unless of course your dream is to become a brain surgeon. Hang around people who are doing what you want to do and be willing to work cheap . . . or for nothing! Sean "P. Diddy" Combs didn't just wake up one day and realize he was one of the most successful record producers in the world. He hung around the recording industry and learned everything he could. And now he *is* the recording industry.

And finally, failure in TV taught me to ask for help from people who know what the heck they are doing. In my distress as a host-director-producer-editor-salesman, I called on a friend, Darlene Hayes, who was a producer on the Phil Donahue show in Chicago. She couldn't save *Ebony/Jet Showcase*, but seeing how much she knew made me realize how much I didn't know, and there's no shame in that. When I returned to radio I hired writers and comedians to make me better, and most of them are still with me in some capacity today, even Darlene!

Becoming the first black man to have a nationally syndicated network morning radio program was a dream of mine that I didn't even realize I'd had. My first real radio job was in Montgomery, Alabama, in the news department at WRMA-AM. A friend of mine, Tracy Larkin, also known as "the Voice," told me about it. Well, that was my first "real," real job in radio, but before that I had a Saturday show at the radio station in Tuskegee. It was the outgrowth of a protest march I'd participated in back in the days when instead of watching cartoons or *Soul Train* on Saturday morning, kids like me marched against segregation. In fact, children were a huge part of the civil rights movement. Our parents, most of whom worked, just couldn't afford to take the chance of being thrown in jail and losing their jobs. So, at some point, they began to send the children out to protest some of the things they deemed unfair. Not to say that the adults hadn't done their share of righting wrongs in Tuskegee. For example, even though the town was 99 percent black, only 1 percent of the businesses were owned by blacks. So, before the much better known Montgomery boycott took place, black Tuskegeans boycotted all the stores and shops in the town until a change was made. But on this particular day it was the children who lined up in front of the town's one radio station to protest the fact that it played only white music. We're talking about being in the heyday of soul music and not being able to hear the Temptations, James Brown, or Wilson Pickett! This was totally unacceptable.

I would love to tell you that it was my love for black music and my sense of duty to my race that brought me to these marches. But in all honesty, it was the peanut butter and jelly sandwiches that were always served to sustain us throughout the day. I was a fat kid, and a good sandwich was just the incentive I needed to become an advocate for change. The white owner of the station decided he didn't need the grief and announced to the crowd he was willing to play black music from noon to sundown on Saturdays. He asked if anyone was interested in doing the job and the hand of mine that wasn't holding the sandwich shot up in the air. I got the job and have been in radio ever since, but I wasn't yet a live deejay.

The station was automated and I learned how to operate the equipment that played the format that I designed. Now, this wasn't the sophisticated automation that we know today. At one point, I decided I could make a little more money if I made tapes of the music shows I'd formatted and sold them to other automated stations. After researching the situation, I discovered that there were about five stations outside of our area that could have used my service. My mom, nicknamed Buddy and always my biggest supporter, helped me compose a business proposal to send to the stations. None of them were interested and I never thought about it again.

A few years ago, however, my daddy found my original letter. When I read it after forty years, I realized that what I had actually been proposing to those five stations was syndication. Buddy and I had an idea that was far ahead of its time but she never lived to see me reach that goal.

I continued with my Saturday afternoon music show until Tracy hooked me up at WRMA in Montgomery. I'd get up every morning and drive an old blue Ford forty-nine miles down the road and do my job, which consisted of "ripping and reading" the news for $90 a week. After a while I got bored with just reading the boring news on the old AP teletype machines, so I started making up my own stories.

You might say I was an early tabloid journalist. Unfortunately, management was not so fond of my style and suggested that I become, instead of a newsman, a deejay. I got addicted right away. I liked talking, I liked joking, and I liked the connection local radio had to the community. Like black newspapers, black radio had a very distinct audience that was rarely visited by "outsiders." But unlike black newspapers, radio was immediate and people could tune in and be constantly and instantly updated about news and information concerning marches, boycotts, or sit-ins. All that from comforting, familiar voices of people you felt like you knew. Top that off with the music you loved, wanted to hear, and would choose as the soundtrack of your life. Who doesn't remember what was playing on the radio on the way to the rally, or the big game, or the funeral? I'm talking about before 8-tracks and cassette players and CDs, and iPods and satellite radio. I'm talking about you inside your car with your black AM soul station. Has anything since been so pertinent and personal? Not for me.

The *Tom Joyner Morning Show*, though it's syndicated in more than 120 markets, is really just a "stepped-up" local radio show with a bigger audience, bigger guests, bigger promotions. Bigger dreams. We try to do on a larger scale what the AM soul stations did during the civil rights movement. Familiarity, compassion, news and information, some laughs, and music you want to hear.

What some people still don't realize about the *Tom Joyner Morning Show* is that even though it has a local feel from city to city, it is not run like a local radio show at all. It's more like *Good Morning America* or the *Today* show—a national morning network show that just happens to be on the radio. It's also the place to be if you want to reach black America. Every morning we talk to more than eight million African Americans in more than 120 markets.

Although the *Tom Joyner Morning Show* had its skeptics early on, I knew it was going to be a success ... or let's say I knew it *had* to be a success. If you truly believe in your dream you can *make* it happen. In fact, making it happen was sort of the underlying theme of our show when it was first launched. In the beginning we faced lots of hurdles. Oh, it's easy to get big names like Denzel, Oprah, and President Clinton to come on our show *now*. In fact big ballers like Clinton and Jimmy Carter, Oprah, and former big ballers like John Kerry and Al Gore call us up when they want to get a message out to black America. But back in the day when we had to really sell who we were, it wasn't easy persuading people to get up early enough to be interviewed on the show ... especially if they were in L.A., where there the show starts at 3 a.m.! We sometimes have to remind guests that they're going to be heard by a huge national audience and it would be a good idea if they got out of bed to do the interview, or at least sat up! As I said, we're very similar to a morning TV show, but we sometimes don't get the same kind of respect. We don't expect full wardrobe and makeup, but, please, no yawning during an interview, Queen Latifah!

I am grateful to people like Luther Vandross, Gladys Knight, Paul Mooney, and others who got on board before the show had proven to be a winner. Others needed much more convincing. "Make it happen!" I'd yell to the show's first publicist Yolanda Starks. And somehow she did.

AS I told you, I'd been dreaming about having my own nationally syndicated morning show for a while, so I came loaded with ideas. That's why dreaming is so great. You don't necessarily know how you're going to make your dreams come true, but when they do come true, you ought to be ready. I was! Nearly ten years ago during a meeting I told my staff I wanted a traveling radio show that would allow us to take huge musical acts from town to town. They were silent. Surely they were thinking to themselves "It Can't Be Done." Sometimes it's hard to get other people to see your dream. A lot of times it's simply because your dream is not their dream. There are people who came on board the *Tom Joyner Morning Show* early, believing that the show they signed on for would be the show they'd be working on for years to come. Those people didn't know me that well. The people who did know me well knew that the *Tom Joyner Morning Show* would continue to evolve and get bigger and better for as long as I was connected with it. If you're planning to be a success in business and in life, I suggest you keep your eyes and ears open for the next big thing. If you don't, there are people out there who will take what you have started, improve it, and turn it into their own.

Eventually the traveling show I had envisioned became the *Southwest Airlines Sky Show*. About thirty times a year our entire crew hits the road and puts on a live party in one of the cities where our show is heard. Musical guests and comedians have included Al Green, Mark Curry, Chaka Khan, A.J. Jamal, Bill Cosby, Brian McKnight, Jill Scott, Earth, Wind & Fire, Adele Givens, Patti LaBelle, New Edition, Dennis Edwards and the Temptations Review, Parliament Funkadelic, Rick James, Erykah Badu, almost every old-school act you can imagine, Cameo, the Ohio Players, the Gap Band, Con-Funkshun . . . the list goes on and on.

If I'm giving the impression that the *Tom Joyner Morning Show* is all about partying, let me make some clarifications. We do party, but we party with a purpose. I just understand that the purpose goes down a lot smoother when a party is attached. The voter registration drives, radio advocacy campaigns, raising money for Historically Black Colleges and Universities, granting Christmas wishes, and keeping black folks abreast of news, issues, and information that is pertinent to our lives is what we always will be about.

As much as I dreamed and continued to dream, I realized I also had to get up and take the steps necessary toward making those dreams a reality. Dreaming is great, but dreaming by itself is not enough. You've got to work hard, know your craft, and know your competition. If you think you'll get far and stay on top without putting everything you've got into it, dream on!

chapter two

"Got Me Working Day and Night"

There is no room for jealousy
in business. If someone is
doing a better job than you
are, either find a way to
improve yourself or join
forces with that person.

I'VE WORKED for most of my life, but it took me a while to realize the benefits of working hard. Even though my hometown of Tuskegee was full of hardworking black men and women. Like most children, I started out trying to get away with doing as little as possible. My daddy noticed this trait in me and quickly let me know that a job half done was not acceptable. The worst beating, I mean spanking, I ever got as a child was after my dad found out I had not delivered all of the papers I was supposed to deliver on my paper route. This was back before you'd go to jail for putting bruises on your children. I ended up going to the family doctor, and when I told him why my daddy had injured me, the family doctor hit me too. That's the way things were in Tuskegee. It took a village to whip a child!

Later I worked at the Veterans Administration hospital in the mental ward. I always say that this is the job that prepared me most for my current job in radio. I actually enjoyed working with the mental patients and we entertained one another. My daddy, who got me the job, worked at the VA hospital for several years until he retired. The VA hospital in Tuskegee was for colored soldiers who had been wounded in World War II. They were good enough to fight for their country but not good enough to be treated in a hospital run by white people. My mom, who worked on campus, had the title of a secretary but actually she was a great writer. She would take her boss's work and make it look good. She also earned extra money redoing and typing theses for doctoral candidates at Tuskegee. She never earned a doctorate herself, but she sure deserved one considering all of the A papers she helped write for other people.

While I was a student at Tuskegee I participated in work-study, which meant I was allowed to earn minimum wage working on campus as long as I worked no more than fifteen hours per week. I convinced my Aunt Nettie, who ran the cafeteria, to let me play the records for the lunch and dinner crowd. I loved it because I was getting paid for combining two of my favorite pastimes—listening to music and eating.

I also found a way to make extra money late in the evening by selling something that my fellow students needed and couldn't get anywhere else. I picked it up, I packaged it and distributed it, and once they got a hold of it, they couldn't get enough. That's right, I was a dealer—of chicken crumbs. One day after eating at the local chicken shack, The Coop, I wondered what the cooks did with all the little crumbs that were left in the grease after the chicken was sold. The answer was, they threw them out. I asked if I could have them. I put them in individual bags and sold them for a quarter. Now trying to sell a bag of chicken crumbs to someone with a full stomach wouldn't be a good business venture at all. But trust me when I tell you business was booming late at night in the dormitory once the cafeteria closed!

You see, once a child has it in his head that he can earn money by providing a service, it never leaves him. For some kids, the desire to work hard and earn an honest living leads to the creation of inventions that have changed the world. For me, I made some extra change selling chicken crumbs.

I don't believe you can put a child to work too young. As soon as a baby begins to walk, he should start working. He can put away his toys, he can empty wastebaskets, he can even sell his own artwork. (Hey, *you're* the one who said it was beautiful!) Show me a spoiled, lazy, bored child and I'll show you a kid without a job. Nobody appreciates playtime more than a kid who works. Once I had children of my own, I put them to work as soon as possible. Most parents use their children's social security numbers for identification purposes. My boys needed their social security numbers so they could get employment! They had chores around the house to do until they were old enough to get jobs as bag boys at the local grocery store. It was there they learned the importance of tipping. And here's a tip for you: Even though your grocery store management will say tipping bag boys is not expected or encouraged, tip them anyway . . . especially if you don't want cracked eggs!

Kids don't really want to work, especially in the summertime when they see their friends kicking back having fun. But you shouldn't make decisions as a parent based on what your children want. The jobs my boys had as teens taught them responsibility, a work ethic, and the value of a dollar, not to mention all of the mysteries of the grocery store—like what the butcher really does when he goes through those swinging doors.

Unlike me, my boys had a chance to see their father work very hard and become successful at something he really loved. My daddy worked hard, but I think he didn't love his profession as an accountant. Fortunately, my brother, Albert, and I have been able to share our lives with him. Taking him with me to South Africa and to see Tiger Woods compete in the Masters Tournament are just a couple of ways we've been able to thank him for teaching us the value of hard work. Pops didn't have the opportunity to make a living pursuing his passion, but he was man enough to make a living anyway, which brings me to another point. There's a lot of talk these days about discovering your passion and getting paid for doing what you love. If you're a young, single person with no children and you don't owe your mama any money, I urge you to try to figure out what you love and find a way to get paid for it. But if you owe your creditors, your parents, your children, or your "baby mama," what you need is a J-O-B! Your passion should be to settle what you owe and to provide your family with everything they need. If you truly have a gift or talent it will still be there after you get your bills together.

On the other hand, passion is a great motivator. The thing you really enjoy doing should move you toward finding a way to make it happen. Otherwise, many of us would just be stuck doing the very first thing we got paid for. Thank goodness there was no future in selling chicken crumbs! Selling wasn't my passion anyway—music and entertainment were. After it became clear that the DuPonts and Commodores were not going to put their massive careers on hold while I finished college at Tuskegee, I needed to figure out how I could combine music, running my mouth, and lack of fashion sense into a career that would sustain me.

I work hard not because I'm trying to live up to my name as the Hardest Working Man in Radio. I work hard because when I was a kid there was a consequence for being lazy—and it was painful. The discipline I received paid off. I've never missed a day of work just because I didn't feel like showing up, and as an employer, I don't expect my employees to shrug off their jobs either. I believe there's no such thing as an insignificant job if you're on someone's payroll. You should always contribute all that you have to every task you take on. Even if you aren't appreciated by your boss you should get some satisfaction in knowing that you've done a job well. More importantly, giving it all you've got gets you in the habit of working hard—a habit that will put you head and shoulders above the rest.

Most people try to do the minimum at their job with the goal of simply avoiding termination. That is not a formula for success, and if it has been your attitude toward working, today is your day to make a change. Believe me, I've been in the position where I had to make a choice—do I play around and do the minimum like everyone else, or do I do what I know is right and work hard? At one point I landed a job in Memphis, at station WLOK which was right down the street from the infamous Lorraine Motel where Dr. King was assassinated. The entire city was filled with the influence of R&B. It was the home of the Stax label and in the early '70s Stax was to R&B funk what Motown was to pop music. Their roster included Isaac Hayes, Al Green, the Bar-Kays, Rufus Thomas, and the Staple Singers. I worked the midday shift from ten to two. Everything was going well until a fellow deejay, who was being fired, pulled a publicity stunt that angered the station owner so much everyone got fired, including me! After just six months I was out of work. Luckily, the general manager, who had also gotten the boot, got a job in St. Louis right away, and he hired me to come along too! I think he wouldn't have considered hiring me if I hadn't already shown myself to be an asset of some kind. In other words, someone is always watching you and if you're doing the right thing, they'll want you to join their team. I can't tell you how many people I've hired that had proven their productivity years before I actually called them up. Sometimes they had worked for me and sometimes they had done a good job for someone else. Either way, I was watching them, and when I've found a slot I thought they could fill, I've offered them a job. There are some people who have been asking me for jobs for years and I unfortunately haven't found a spot for them yet. They may not believe it, but when it becomes available, the job is theirs.

The key is to keep being productive and not to give up just because you think you're not getting that golden opportunity you feel you deserve. This includes sometimes doing a job that you may feel is beneath you. The "it's not my job" mind-set never sits well with employers. If your boss asks you to do it, and it's not illegal or immoral—it's your job!

In a world where, for many young people, it's all about the "bling," where rappers brag about their money and their fleet of cars, telling a kid to work hard and be willing to do the grunt work is not an easy sell. That's why you shouldn't wait until they're eighteen to start talking to them about work. If they begin taking out the trash, mowing the lawn, raking the neighbors' leaves, washing and waxing cars, selling home-made crafts, etc. when they're kids, they won't look at you like you're crazy when you suggest that they accept an entry-level position at a company.

If you really want to motivate young people, you have to hit them where they live. Don't tell them to get to work on time, show up every day, give it their best, never steal from the cash register, just so that they can someday become executives and retire comfortably—that goal means absolutely nothing to a twelve-year-old boy. Instead, tell him if he does all those things, he'll end up with the fine women.

It was in St. Louis that I really learned the value of working hard and doing stuff no one else was willing to do. The best thing about St. Louis was there was so much live entertainment. There was always something going on. Groups and performers would pass through town and the Carousel Hotel would get them to perform in the ballroom. The hotel had a trade-out agreement with the radio station, which meant the hotel could get commercials on our radio station in trade for rooms at the hotel. So, a lot of deejays (who shall remain nameless) had their girlfriends staying at the hotel. They would throw parties with artists such as Archie Bell and the Drells, Carlos Santana, and James Brown. The station, because of all kinds of accounting problems and mismanagement of funds, was in a lot of debt; it had gotten so bad that the station manager didn't have a checking account and we got paid in cash on Fridays at lunchtime while I was on the air. The staff would get their money and head over to the hotel for hours. There would be no one left in the entire station on Friday afternoon except me. I was supposed to get off the air at two o'clock but sometimes whoever was supposed to go on the air next wouldn't get back until four or five o'clock. There would be no receptionist to answer the phone calls and that was back before there were answering machines and voice mail. So, I spun records and ran the station.

After three months of that I got a call from Chuck Smith from radio station KKDA-AM in Dallas with a job offer. He had heard me on the air while driving through St. Louis. He thought I sounded confident on the air, but actually I was just busy. I did whatever I had to do at the station except do maintenance on the transmitter, and I would have done that too if necessary.

That hard work in St. Louis paid off because Chuck Smith offered me the most important time slot in radio—mornings. No matter what kind of job you have, there are going to be some people who like to screw up. They have no work ethic, don't care about punctuality, and do as little work as possible. Their lack of motivation can be good for you if you're a hard worker, because nine times out of ten if you get to work on time, are willing to stay late, do a good job, and are always looking for a way to make yourself and your company look good, it will pay off. You still might get fired, but you will rise again. Someone like me or Chuck Smith has been watching you and is waiting to give you a chance to prove what you can do.

The only explanation I have for not leaving early after getting my check on Fridays and going to the picnics with the rest of the station employees was that those beatings I got for doing a poor job as a paperboy really stuck. If I was being paid to do a job, I did it. I also needed my radio job and I figured if there was no station, there would be no me, so it was in my best interest to try to keep it running. Sure, I got fired anyway, but even that turned out to be a blessing.

Chances are you won't begin any profession at the top whether you strive to be a deejay, a ditchdigger, or an analyst on Wall Street, and, yes, they get fired too! And often, those who do rise to the top aren't necessarily the brightest, the flashiest, or the ones who believed they knew it all. Those who rise to the top of their game—and stay there—are usually the ones who are willing to work their asses off.

By the way, guess what happened to that radio station in St. Louis? When the Mississippi River swelled up one spring, the whole building floated away. If I had been on the air that day, I would have gone with it, straight down the Mississippi. And if it had happened on a Friday afternoon, I would have been there all by myself.

WHEN MY son Thomas asked me what this book would be about, and I said that among other things it would include tips on becoming a good employee by working hard, he looked at me with amazement. "Dad, didn't you tick off most of the people you worked for?" Out of the mouths of thirty-year-olds!

He got me. I did tick off most of the people I worked for, including my son Oscar, who is now my boss! But in my defense, when I ticked off an employer, it was usually because I was trying hard to do something that I thought was a great idea—and they were trying hard to stop me from doing it.

For example, there was the time I accepted two radio jobs in two separate states and had to travel daily from Dallas, where I did a morning show, to Chicago, where I did an afternoon show. It worked out in the end because I got tons of publicity, not to mention great ratings for both radio stations. But it took a minute for my bosses, who each initially thought I'd be working for him exclusively, to warm up to the idea.

Then there was the time I claimed on the air that someone had stolen my "air" guitar. I may have taken it too far when I called the Dallas police and actually reported the theft. For some reason the cops got upset when they had to come down to the station and listen to me give a description of my imaginary bass, and they arrested me.

Then there was the time we were having a problem with a sponsor and I was told that if I mentioned the name on the air I'd be fired. So, as soon as the show came on the air, I said the name over and over in the first twenty seconds.

I rarely actually *intend* to upset my employers. It's just important for me to have a certain amount—no, make that a *large* amount—of freedom. I am a child of the civil rights movement after all. One of the reasons radio and the entertainment industry appealed to me in the first place was because of the freedom they allowed me. I'm not a nine-to-five, suit-and-tie kind of guy. In fact, I wear shorts and flip-flops to work for about nine months out of the year. I do my best thinking not behind a desk but on a lounge chair on the beach or—and let me warn you, this isn't pretty—at home naked with candles burning.

When something exciting pops into my head, I notify whatever member of my staff I feel can make it happen the quickest. Now, remember, I haven't always had a staff. Back in the day when I got an exciting idea, I would notify my own self and then try to sell it to my boss, who was usually the program director of the radio station. But it seems to me, the problem with most program directors, bosses, supervisors, etc. is that their favorite word is "no." That's a word I've never liked to hear, so early on in my career I figured out that the easiest way to keep from hearing "no" is to not ask for permission in the first place. Some of my most successful promotions started out with a lot of resistance from people who couldn't see my vision. But if *I* can see it, I'm going to do everything I can to make it happen. Often without the blessings of management.

This may not be the best way to make points on the job, but it is a testament to one's efforts to keep coming up with fresh, innovative ways of doing things.

When I became a boss, I often looked for people who had pulled off big things. When I attend large, successful events, I often seek out the person who put them together and try to get that person to join our team.

You should always be willing to see the greatness in others. I found out very early that a lot of people are just the opposite. When others do something well, it's sometimes difficult for people to give them their props and to admit that someone else just might be superior. That's crazy to me. I know that there are a whole lot of people who can do a whole lot of things better than I can, and I want them to be on my team.

There is no room for jealousy in business. If someone is doing a better job than you are, either find a way to improve yourself or join forces with that person. Always keep your eyes and ears open for an opportunity to add another layer to what you already have to offer. I also look for people who have been trying to get where they're going for a while, people who have done internships and apprenticeships, and worked in some entry-level positions in the areas in which they're applying. That tells me about their commitment and willingness to learn from the ground up. You wouldn't believe how many young people I meet who want to get *paid* before they've proven that they can do anything.

If you think you're a good writer or a good producer and you're trying to get some experience, make getting experience your priority. Don't expect to be paid just because you think you know how to do something. Expect to get paid when what you know how to do is something that is needed. You cannot be certain that someone needs you just because you're ready for a job. But you *can* be ready when a job you're able to do becomes available. You never know when the call will come! In the meantime, keep brushing up and getting better.

Show me a person who doesn't mess up and I'll show you a person who isn't doing anything. I hate baseball, but I do have a good baseball analogy that I can't let go to waste: The best hitters on any team are the ones who have the most strike-outs. (By the way, the reason I hate baseball is because it's too slow. Anytime a sport has a designated moment for you to stand up and stretch, you know it's boring! In baseball there's no time limit, no cheerleaders, and in place of a band they have an organist.) But back to my point, as long as you're trying to accomplish something, you're going to make mistakes. What most bosses hate much more than mistakes are excuses, especially before the problem has been rectified. When something goes wrong on the job, the first thing you should do is correct it or tell your boss what steps you plan to take to make the problem go away. When you try to explain why it happened—and even worse why it isn't your fault—you're not helping the situation and you sound defensive and petty.

I've made my share of mistakes throughout my career. One

of my biggest ones haunted me for a long time. Years ago, a record company rep brought a young woman to the radio station and asked if I could spend a few moments talking to her. I had some other things scheduled for the show and told the rep I couldn't squeeze the newcomer in. The rep assured me that this woman was going to be the hottest thing out there and I would regret not interviewing her. The rep was absolutely right. The young woman was Whitney Houston and I think she still holds a grudge against me even now, which I don't think is right. If she can forgive Bobby, surely she can forgive me!

No matter what your job status is, whether you're climbing the corporate ladder, flipping burgers, or running a company, you can always learn more about becoming better at what you do. One thing I continue to do is read about people who have accomplished great things, especially in business, and I suggest that you do the same. There's nothing wrong with emulating the good habits of people who are successful. And it's inspiring to learn about some of the challenges they've gone through. For me, reading a biography or autobiography is a much better use of time than reading a novel. Some of my favorites have been about Muhammad Ali, Sammy Davis Jr., Aretha Franklin, The Rock, Berry Gordy Jr., Smokey Robinson, Chaka Khan, and Bob Johnson. I can hear it now: *"You actually count a book about the wrestler 'The Rock' as one of your favorite biographies?"* I absolutely do. And if you've decided to discount The Rock or anyone else who has become a success in his field, without knowing that person's story, you could be missing out on something that could help you in some way.

Maybe that's one of the benefits of having been a C-minus student in school—I believe that there are some pretty ordinary people who have some extraordinary things to say. It's also helped me to look for something in my employees that

many overlook—it's called *heart*. I have a lot of people working for me and doing an excellent job who might have had a
tough time getting hired in similar positions at other companies. I don't have a perfect record but, more often than not, I
can spot a person who is ready to prove to me and the world
that she can do a great job. I think it's a trait I inherited from
my mother who saw something good in most people and saw
some good in me before anyone else did. If you're a boss, take
a chance on somebody sometimes.

The one book that has inspired me the most and I have
reread several times is *Succeeding Against the Odds* by John H.
Johnson. I read it when I'm feeling good and I read it when
I'm feeling bad. It reminds me of what I'm doing right and
what I'm doing wrong. It also reminds me of something that
most of us forget—failure doesn't mean the end, but quitting
does. We know John H. Johnson as one of the richest men in
the world and the head of one of the world's most successful
businesses: Johnson Publishing in Chicago. We all know
Ebony and *Jet* magazines but how many of us know about the
Negro Digest? It was the precursor to the other two publica-
tions.

When Mr. Johnson was a young child, his mom moved
him from a small town in Arkansas to Chicago, where against
the odds this country boy who was teased unmercifully for his
southern dialect excelled in school and studied journalism at
Northwestern University. When he began his first publishing
business he never lost track of who his audience was and made
absolutely no apologies for his undying commitment to serve
black consumers.

When I went to work for John H. Johnson as a deejay at his
radio station in Chicago in the '70s, one of the things I learned
is no matter how big you think you are, you need to be personally involved in the daily operations of your own business.

No one cares about what you have as much as you do, and when things go wrong, no one stands to lose more than you. It's ultimately up to the boss to make sure everyone is doing the job he's been hired to do.

Since I am the Hardest Working Man in Radio, if you work for me, expect to work hard too. Here a few things that I always expect from my employees:

• When you don't feel like working, don't let me know about it. Enthusiasm goes a very long way with me. I love people who love to do a good job and people only do a good job when they're where they want to be. It took me a while to figure this out, but you should never beg a person to come to work for you. People who have to be sold on your company are usually the least loyal and much more likely to leave when another opportunity comes their way. Being on a job is like being in a relationship: There are mutual agreements and there should be mutual respect. But there should also be excitement, spontaneity, and continuous growth.

• Don't take your position for granted. Keep bringing new and interesting things to the table, and don't always wait for the boss to ask for them. Show me that you're as interested in having and keeping your job today as you were the first day you were hired. Impress me. There's an old saying: Don't stay at the party too long. The longer you just hang around the less attractive you become. Sometimes it's like that on a job. If you're just staying because there's nothing else and nowhere else to go, you are becoming complacent. Find a way to shake things up by giving your position a face-lift. You don't have to wait for your boss or supervisor to suggest it. Create another layer to your position that will make the job and you look more interesting. Don't necessarily expect more money, but, if it's an asset to the company, your boss may recognize it at raise

time, and if not, it will look good on your résumé when you're
looking for your next job.

I chose to work in a career where business attire isn't a pre-
requisite; however, there are times when even I have to wear
hard-soled shoes and a tie. If you're interviewing for a job,
even if it's for lifeguard, wear shoes, a shirt or blouse, some decent pants, dress, or skirt. And unless you're trying out for the
NBA, or the WNBA for that matter, don't show up for the interview in cornrows. Once you're hired, take your cue from
the people around you.

Don't feel too bad, though, if you've mistakenly shown up
to a job wearing inappropriate clothing, because you're in
good company. My good friend Ed Gordon, formerly of BET,
got a job on the news staff at MSNBC. Ed, who is fond of pas-
tel colors, didn't really fit in with the more conservatively
dressed on-air staff at MSNBC. Later when he landed a job at
60 Minutes I warned him to tone down his suits. My advice to
him was to follow Morley Safer's lead. "If Morley doesn't wear
gators and a pumpkin-colored suit, neither should you, Ed." I
give you the same advice. Check out what your boss or supervisor is wearing and dress accordingly.

I think we have the best group of employees in the world
at our company. And since I'm just a deejay, I'm pretty lax
about a dress code. Jeans, midriff tops, cornrows, twists, dreds,
perms, weaves, shaved heads, press and curls, Afros, all are
represented and welcome. However, if you show up with a
freeze hairstyle or a high-top fade, you will get talked about!
The bottom line is our team works hard and the people are
fun to be around. We work together and we party together
and that takes a very delicate balance. There are a lot of smart,
talented, loyal people out there, but that isn't always enough.
If you're all of that plus you can reenact a scene from the

movie *Blazing Saddles,* drink shots of tequila, sing karaoke until dawn with the person who authorizes your time sheet and respect yourself and your boss on Monday morning, plus remember to work hard every day, send me your résumé.

chapter Three

"The Big Payback"

If I learned anything in my
hometown of Tuskegee, it was
the importance of giving
back. We were a community in
every sense of the word, and
the better off your neighbor
was, the better off
you were, too.

GROWING UP in a town like Tuskegee and seeing a community run by progressive black people made me believe there was nothing I couldn't accomplish if I had the will to make it happen. No one actually told me there was nothing I could not do, but somehow the message got to me and the other kids I grew up with like Lionel Richie and hundreds more you may have never heard of but who have gone on to do extraordinary things. There were people such as Sonny Boy, who had hundreds of patents on his inventions and for years worked in the space program at NASA. A lot of monkeys shot into space were Sonny Boy's. Big-Head Grant helped build the original NASA tracking system in Huntsville. He was the TV repairman in our town. Doc, who was a commercial artist, is still in jail because his illegal drug factory blew up.

It wasn't until after I left Tuskegee that I realized I didn't have the typical African American experience. I would later meet black people who thought certain jobs, professions, incomes, and lifestyles were out of their reach just because of the color of their skin. And the weird part is I was raised in one of the most segregated states in the country before all of the gains of the civil rights movement! I know I'm just a deejay, but it didn't take me long to realize that somewhere along the way, black folks had gotten it twisted.

Why was it, I wondered, that black people who grew up in

a more "mainstream" environment often were plagued with self-doubt? What was it about growing up in a town like mine, being educated by, nurtured by, and slapped upside the head by people who had nothing but your best interest in mind that made your life better? It wasn't rocket science. Our community was a reflection of Tuskegee Institute, and Tuskegee Institute, like the other HBCUs, took black children and turned them into confident, caring, committed African American adults. Even though as a kid I might not have consciously realized what native heroes Tuskegee Airman Daniel "Chappie" James, Booker T. Washington, Rosa Parks, and many others contributed, their can-do spirit was present and I think most people who lived there felt it too. It inspired us in many ways. But mostly that can-do spirit made us proud, and it made us productive. We challenged ourselves to see just how far we could get.

If I learned anything in my hometown of Tuskegee, it was the importance of giving back. We were a community in every sense of the word, and the better off your neighbor was, the better off you were too. "Mentoring" wasn't a word I heard as a kid, but when I look back I can see I was surrounded by people I admired and looked up to. Even though they never called themselves "role models" or "mentors," they absolutely were. Rev. Kenneth L. Buford was more than the pastor of my church when I was growing up. He was president of the local NAACP and was active in the civil rights movement. He didn't just preach to us from a pulpit; his life and his actions outside of the church are what had an impact on me.

Chappie James would fly his fighter plane real low when he got over our town and everyone would look up and say, "There goes Chappie!" The pride and honor we felt was indescribable.

Rev. Raymond Harvey wasn't the pastor of our church, but

sometimes, because our friends and family were members of his congregation, I'd get to hear him preach. I thought he was a great speaker and I aspired to be able to hold an audience's attention the way he did. In fact, when I was a kid there were only two people whose sermons I'd always stay awake for: Rev. Harvey and a visiting preacher we'd have at our church from time to time by the name of Rev. Martin Luther King Jr.

Alberta Richie, my eighth-grade teacher, was a wonderful, compassionate person who made even a C-minus student like me feel better about school. And aside from being one of my favorite teachers, she was also my good friend Lionel's mom. Mrs. Richie was sweet enough to pass me to the ninth grade, even though I'd missed thirteen weeks of school after breaking my hip playing football. I was hospitalized for a period of time and was in a body cast. It was a horrible experience. The cast made me sweat and itch and I was immobile. I wasn't doing all that great in school before I left, and I missed a whole lot while I was gone. Still, that sweet Mrs. Richie gave me a passing grade.

Years later, I got to wondering whether she passed me solely because of her good heart or for another reason. Lionel, or "Skeet" as we called him, was in her class too and he struggled in school just as much as I did. Maybe she feared that if she flunked me, she would have to flunk him too. We both matriculated, and if any school board officials want to challenge it, it's too late now!

Because of Mrs. Richie, I'll always have a special place in my heart for schoolteachers. Every once in a while on the *Morning Show,* we'll pay tribute to educators by asking listeners to name the schoolteacher that made the biggest difference in their lives. There's never any shortage of callers, which confirms my belief that teaching is a profession made up of unsung heroes who make a difference and the influence they have on their students can be long lasting. Too few teachers get their due.

My neighbors, teachers, and preachers were examples of what you could become if you worked hard, treated people right, went to school, and, most importantly, gave something back. Chief Charles Alfred Anderson was considered the father of black aviators. From childhood he was fascinated with flying, but since most flight instructors in the 1900s would not take black students, he taught himself to fly at age twenty-two.

By 1932 he had his commercial pilot's license and began taking history-making long-distance flights. In 1940 Tuskegee Institute hired him as its chief flight instructor and he developed a pilot-training program for the school. A flight instructor who helped start the Tuskegee Airman program, he later taught a whole lot of black people in Tuskegee how to fly planes.

You just didn't see a lot of Negroes flying planes in the 1940s and 1950s, but the ones you saw flying in Alabama who weren't Tuskegee Airmen probably learned from the chief. He was still teaching people to fly in the 1980s when he died.

I witnessed a lot of Chappie's kind of selflessness as a kid. Some of us are so worried about getting ahead, we often don't have time to see who may be following in our footsteps. Often those people need a little hand, or a boost, or in my case specifically a passing grade! It makes a difference.

One Hundred Black Men is an organization that's dedicated to providing mentors for kids. The Boys & Girls Clubs of America and Big Brothers Big Sisters are also excellent places to go if you'd like to become a mentor or are looking for one. But remember, in order to make a difference, you don't *have* to join a group. I promise you that if you're living your life right, or wrong for that matter, there's some young person watching and emulating your behavior. With that in mind, do the right thing. And remember, showing is better than talking.

I also know for a fact that growing up seeing other black people doing big things was much more meaningful to me than seeing white people doing big things. Yet Secretary of State and Alabama homie Condoleezza Rice doesn't seem to agree with me. In an article in *Essence* magazine a few years ago, the then national security adviser told an interviewer, "I never believed the argument that you have to see somebody who looks like you in order to do something. If that were so, there wouldn't be any firsts." In other words, I guess she meant she still was able to rise to the powerful positions she's held without having seen any other sisters in those roles. That is true. But there will be a lot more little black girls believing they can reach the heights she has reached simply because Condoleezza's there.

Basketball great Irvin "Magic" Johnson is a hero of mine. After retiring from the NBA he became a business mogul and placed most of his emphasis on the "hood": Inner-city areas that most business investors would run from became his targets. In the end, it was a "win-win-win" situation for Magic, the businesses, and the community.

Magic Johnson has improved areas like the Baldwin Hills section of Los Angeles by opening a movie theater in the once-thriving community and turning it into one of the most profitable in the country. I know people who drive thirty miles away from home to patronize the Magic Johnson Theatre because they know it's good for the hood. Magic didn't stop there. He also opened Starbucks in black neighborhoods and they're the places to be if you're looking to meet other African Americans who have enough money for an expensive cup of latte! Whenever Magic was on our show we'd joke that two of the most expensive things out there are movie popcorn and

Starbucks coffee and he's selling both. Magic didn't stop with L.A. He's got businesses all over the country. He believes black people don't want to drive out of their neighborhoods to go to a movie or buy gourmet coffee, and he believes that if he provides a good service to the community the community will support him. Is anybody mad at Magic for doing what no one was willing to do and making millions along the way? I don't think so. Magic took a big gamble and won; at the same time he made a difference. If you've benefited from the sacrifices others have made to improve your life, it's time to decide what you can do to make a difference in the lives of others. You may not be able to do what Magic Johnson has done but you can do something. Become a mentor or a volunteer in a local election. Collect winter coats for the homeless or work in a soup kitchen. These are all things you can do right now. It's time for the big payback. It's a check that will never bounce.

chapter four

It's a Black Thang
(and if you don't understand, so what!)

*"You're a young smart Negro.
I'm an old smart Negro,"
John H. Johnson would yell at
me. "I've got to know more
than you do!"*

WHEN I worked in the news department at WRMA-AM in Montgomery, Alabama, one of my duties was to attend press conferences at the state capitol. It was a stretch for me to be working in the news department in the first place. I hadn't had any training in journalism and there I was surrounded by real reporters with real questions to ask. Back then I had an Afro and I'd usually be sporting a colorful dashiki, and even though I wasn't exactly confident about my reporting skills, I always managed to ask one question and that question never varied. Whether the press conference was about raising state taxes or the upcoming Christmas tree lighting ceremony, my one and only question would always be the same: "What does this mean for black people?" And I meant it too. I meant it then and I mean it now. Everything I've done, everything I do, and everything I continue to work for is for black people. That's all I know. It's in my blood. It's who I am.

My family, teachers, coaches, pastors, friends, enemies, girl-friends, the girls who refused to dance with me, my barber, pediatrician, and dentist were all black. I delivered newspapers to black people, I attended a historically black college, and I joined a black fraternity. I married a black woman and had two black children. During the civil rights movement I walked, marched, boycotted, sat in, and stood up with and for black people. Every job I've held in my adult life was providing some type of service to black people. My first job in radio was an outcome of a protest over the radio station's not playing black music.

Every audience I've ever had has been largely made up of black people. That's not to assume that other races of people aren't listening to—or for that matter reading—what I have to say. But I'm talking specifically to black folks.

Reaching out to black people was something innate because it's what I saw growing up in Tuskegee. Tuskegee Institute, the mother ship of our community, didn't only educate the black students enrolled there, it also nurtured them by serving the students and the whole town a steady diet of consciousness-raising commentary from the leading intellectuals of our time. It was also a center for black culture. It was common for H. Rap Brown, Malcolm X, Leontyne Price, and "the Godfather of Soul" James Brown to make appearances in Tuskegee and we all showed up to support them. Dr. King and Rosa Parks were regular fixtures around town.

We spent a lot of time making efforts to integrate restaurants, schools, and churches because it was the right thing to do, not because we felt that eating alongside, learning alongside, or worshipping alongside white people would make us any more complete than we already were.

When I was hired by the legendary John H. Johnson as a deejay on his Chicago radio station, I learned that what Tuskegee Institute and Johnson Publishing were doing was Super-Serving the black community, and I've been committed to this "religion" ever since.

Mr. Johnson built his entire career creating and perfecting a medium dedicated to highlighting the achievements of black people. Before *Ebony* and *Jet* magazines, black newspapers were the only source for finding out what black people were doing in other parts of the country. *Ebony* and *Jet* were big, with lots of pictures and ads on glossy paper. Black people had never had anything that looked like this and that included people who looked like them. Fashioned after the mainstream *Look* and *Life* magazines, *Ebony* featured black movie stars, athletes, politicians, movers and shakers, and high achievers. Mr. Johnson not only knew his audience, but he also was devoted to his audience and remains so today. His commitment to Super-Serving his readership by providing them with what no one else would provide is unwavering. His constant challenge was convincing advertisers that they were wasting an opportunity when they failed to go after the black consumer. When I worked for Mr. Johnson he would let me know whenever I seemed to be losing my focus on the audience I was supposed to be serving. And he pulled no punches. He knew what he was talking about and he let me know it.

"You're a young smart Negro. I'm an *old* smart Negro," John H. Johnson would yell at me. "I've got to know more than you do!"

Mr. Johnson taught me that it's never necessary to try to reach out to people other than your core audience. If other people like what you do, that's fine, but to deliberately try to cross over to attract white people is detrimental. A lot of black performers learn this the hard way. Some start out with the right idea but get blinded by the perceived ultimate success linked with having gone crossover.

When Luther Vandross began his career in the '80s he hit the ground running with R&B hit after hit. In the '90s his music began to appeal more and more to the white audience and was getting more airplay on "lite," "soft hits," and "easy listening" formats. By the year 2000, Luther was still a huge star but it was clear that his music was less R&B and more "crossover." The core audience that had once run out to buy his CDs as soon as they were released was drying up.

Lionel Richie, Whitney Houston, Mariah Carey, Michael

Jackson, and Janet Jackson all became superstars thanks to the acceptance they received from white audiences. By the way, you're only a "superstar" if white people like you too. But when times get tough and public humiliation, highly publicized personal drama, arrests, drug charges, nervous breakdowns, or wardrobe malfunctions occur, black superstars find their way back home to their black audiences in a hurry. And nine times out of ten, we're there welcoming them with open arms.

We are probably the most forgiving people on the planet. We'll joke about you publicly and talk about you privately, but it's very rare that we will forsake you. In fact, the more white people publicly vilify a black public figure, the more we feel the need to defend that person. Black people forgave former DC mayor Marion Berry, former president Bill Clinton (an honorary brother), and even O.J. Even though we know someone is wrong, we will not stand to see that someone get kicked when he's down. It's a combination of our religious faith and belief in redemption, our role as victims, and somewhere in the back of our minds our knowledge that very likely we'll be the falsely accused or falsely arrested for something at some point in our lives.

Most of us live with the thought and fear that we're going to be set up, and we're always taking precautions. You're never too big to receive your "N word" wake-up call—the message that reminds you that you aren't white, even if you're on the Hollywood A-list, have a white spouse, live in the suburbs, and drive a Mercedes station wagon to soccer practice.

You can get the call in all sorts of ways, like trying to get a cab in New York City, being followed around by a security guard at a department store because you aren't recognized, being pulled over for driving while black. Watch how a black person, who would never have any intention of stealing anything, holds up his or her receipt in a store when exiting. I know a guy who says he always keeps his gas and ATM receipts, not so much to keep track of what he's spent, but because the receipts have the time and date of use printed on them. "You never know when I'll have to prove to the police where I was at a certain time," he said.

I know parents who are leery about having their children fingerprinted even though it could possibly help the kids be recovered if they come up missing. They worry that having their kids' prints on file will somehow make it easier for police to pick them up years down the road. These are the things black people struggle with. They may not share these things with white people but they share them with each other. That's one of the purposes the *Tom Joyner Morning Show* serves. It gives black people a real forum to discuss things that are real to them.

One of the things that annoys and frustrates white people most about me is that I admit that I am broadcasting to black people, I admit that our Web site BlackAmericaWeb.com covers news for black people, and I even admit that the Fantastic Voyage Cruise is for black people. White listeners call me and say, "I like your show, I listen every day and I don't understand why you direct everything toward black people as though no white people are listening." Some of them are angry, some of them are hurt, and almost all of them are white women married to black men. Sometimes I ask them if their husband likes the show, and they usually hesitantly answer yes.

In the aftermath of 9/11, when I told my staff and crew that I wanted to send money to the black victims, some of them took offense. "Tom, this is a time to reach out to American victims, period. We shouldn't single out black victims. It doesn't sound right. We're all Americans, there should be no black or white right now." I understood where they were coming from, but I still believed that we could provide a service to the black victims that they otherwise might not receive.

When the war on terrorism began, we got calls from soldiers all over the world who were fans of the show. One morning a white soldier called to give a shout-out, and when he was done I asked him to put some black soldiers on the phone. That upset some people too. "Tom, it made it seem like you didn't want to talk to the white soldier."

I GET the same type of concern and criticism about raising money for kids who run out of money at Historically Black Colleges and Universities. "Tom, why do you just raise money for HBCUs? Why not help kids no matter what college they attend. It seems like you only want to help kids at *black* colleges, but what about all the other kids at all the other schools who need help?"

Here's the deal: White America is not breaking down the doors to serve black people. I am. Turn on your television, turn on your radio, open up your newspapers and magazines, go to bookstores, go anywhere you want, and I'll tell you what you'll get from white America—as much as it takes to get by to keep black people from complaining, and in most cases that's not much. The goal of the white media is to serve a white audience. That's what they do. They don't call it white, they call it " mainstream," but it means white. They create things that appeal mostly to mainstream audiences. So, when I watched or read mainstream media coverage on 9/11, for example, I saw many, many stories about white victims and a few stories about black victims. When I watched or read mainstream coverage of the war in Iraq, I saw many, many stories about white soldiers and their families back home and a few stories about black soldiers. When I watched and read mainstream coverage of the presidential elections, I saw many, many white people talking about who they would vote for and the issues that were of great concern to them and a few black people expressing their opinions.

If you are white, you probably don't see things this way at all. You may think that we've come so far as a nation and that slavery and racism and all that stuff are over and done with. You probably think we should just move ahead and not think about the color of a person's skin. Okay, fine. You may really believe this but you're probably not the one running things in this country.

You're probably not the person who comes up with the "quotas." Oh, you know about the quotas, don't you? It's funny, because conservatives criticize those of us who are in favor of a quota system. They say everyone should just stand on his own merit. Color should not come into play. But as Rev. Jesse Jackson says, white America has always used the quota system. For example, when corporate America is looking for ten qualified candidates to come up with an advertising campaign, and ten of the five hundred people who show up are qualified African Americans, will all ten of those African Americans get hired? Not in this life. Out of the hundreds of people who would be interviewed I would bet my life that no more than three African Americans would be hired. That's a quota system and it's used all the time. But to most of America it just looks normal. And because it looks normal, America perpetuates the myth that of all of the five hundred people who are interviewed, only two or three blacks are qualified.

African Americans see it all the time. The two or three black anchorpeople on the news in your town, the three or four black actors on your soap opera, the two black doctors on your favorite hospital drama, the two black contestants on the reality show you watch? It's all because of a quota system.

And while we're on the topic of reality shows, let's stay here

for a moment. I'm not a huge fan of them but most of our listeners are. Some days, I feel like we need Dr. Phil, Dr. Alvin
Poussaint, Iyanla Vanzant, and the pope on hand to help black
viewers of reality TV get through the anger and disappointment they feel when a sister or a brother is "undeservedly"
voted off, eliminated, or fired from one of these programs. I'm
always surprised that they are so surprised at some of the out-
comes. I try to brace them for the fall, and even though it
doesn't occur all the time, it occurs enough.

For most of mainstream America, I think watching reality
programs is pure entertainment. For most black Americans
it's a combination of stress, pressure, apprehension, bitterness,
retribution, fear, and strife. Me? I'd rather watch a rerun of
Sanford and Son. Now that's entertainment.

A LOT of black people tend to watch reality TV shows the
same way they watch real life, hoping that something will
change, hoping that mainstream America will all of a sudden
get the desire to make our needs a priority. I'm not one of those
people. I don't expect white America to do what it doesn't
want to do. I'm going to do it myself. Like Mr. Johnson, I
know and love black people enough to believe I can give us
what we want. And what we want is a little different from
what the mainstream wants. If you don't believe me, listen to
our show. Three days a week, on our segment "Express Yourself," we give our audience a chance to express themselves
about particular topics, and if you really want to put your fin-
ger on the pulse of black America, tune in. One Monday we
asked them to name the white TV show everyone is talking
about that they've never watched. *Friends,* which may have
been one of the most popular shows in TV history, was the
winner by an overwhelming margin. Other shows most of our
listeners never ever watch are *Survivor* and *Everybody Loves*

Raymond. Not only didn't they love Raymond, they didn't even like him!

Of course there are exceptions to every rule. Every black person I know watches at least one program that is really "targeted" to mainstream America, and a whole lot of black people I know don't watch any of the shows that are "targeted" toward African Americans. Until those doing the targeting are made up of more people who are a true representation of the black population, there will be a whole lot of hitting and missing going on. Just to produce a show with five or six black people is not enough. There must be good, intelligent writing with dialogue that rings true to its audience. That's not happening on most black television shows today.

The black-white issue is real, and on our show we choose not to ignore it and we try to have fun with it when we ask our audience questions like who's dating a white person on the down low, what's your favorite white singing group, who's the white family who won't move out of the hood, and who is the coolest white person you know? Instead of being offended over the fact that we spend four hours a day talking to black people, I think white people who listen should have fun with it, too. They're getting a chance to hear what we really talk about when they're not around!

We also have fun with topics even when they're not funny at all. I'm a true believer that it's easier to get people informed if they're laughing. You may not be able to find the humor in the *Plessy v. Ferguson* Supreme Court decision, but we did. Homer Plessy, who was one-eighth black, thought he could sit in the first-class section on the train back in 1892 because he bought a first-class ticket. The nerve! He didn't realize that under Louisiana law he was considered black and was required to sit in the "colored" car. Plessy argued he should have been treated like a white man and that the Separate Car Act violated the constitution. But Judge Howard Ferguson said it WAS constitutional and found Plessy guilty of not leaving the whites-only car. My colleague J, who can make a light-skinned–dark-skinned argument out of any topic, immediately inferred that Homer Plessy was a relative of mine and nicknamed him "the train jock." Every day we highlight a "Little Known Black History Fact" because we can't wait until Black History Month in February to start talking about the struggles and accomplishments of black people. The facts aren't always "little known" but when we get through with them they do usually have a new twist.

THERE WAS a time when black people depended on other black people for almost everything we needed—we had to. But just because we had to doesn't mean it was a bad thing. The support we gave each other brought a type of cohesiveness into our communities that we may never witness again.

When people see how much I fight for HBCUs they may not realize the history these institutions have in our country. When the oldest of the Historically Black Colleges and Universities in America—Cheyney University of Pennsylvania—was founded in 1837, this was its mission: to provide free classical education for qualified young people. The college's founder, Richard Humphreys, born on a plantation in the West Indies, charged thirteen Quakers to design an institution to "instruct the descendents of the African race in school learning, in the various branches of the mechanic arts, trades and agriculture, in order to prepare and fit and qualify them to act as teachers." It began as the Institute for Colored Youth and was changed to Cheyney State Teachers College when the campus moved to George Cheyney's farm in 1902, and finally to Cheyney State College in 1959. In 1983 Cheyney became

Cheyney University of Pennsylvania. It was there for black people when nothing else was.

Integration is a wonderful thing, and I'm one of the many who fought for it during the civil rights movement. But integration also caused many to choose to leave our communities. When we left, many of the businesses that had thrived died. Some people are working hard to try to revive our old neighborhoods; some people think it's too late.

Bob Johnson gets a lot of criticism for the content he airs on Black Entertainment Television. His critics say since BET really is THE major cable network catering to African Americans, along with TV-One and MBC, it should strive to feature more positive and original programming. And while I agree there is room for improvement at BET, I've heard Bob Johnson's explanation and I respect it. Bob Johnson never promised that BET would be all things to all black people. Airing black music videos, and doing it inexpensively, was its benchmark and the network remains loyal to that plan. Along the way, to its credit, BET has added some original series, coverage of black college sports, several awards shows, and an impressive nightly news program anchored by Jacque Reid. BET's *Comic View,* a showcase for black comedians, has launched the careers of several comics including D.L. Hughley, Bruce Bruce, and our favorite white comedian, Gary Owen.

I, like most black people I know, did always hope that he would eventually add some black programs that would compete with what we were getting from the networks; and when Bob sold BET to media giant Viacom for $3 billion, I thought things might change for the better. Now BET was owned by a huge company that had money and resources and a very powerful white man at the helm, Mel Karmazin. When one of the first actions BET took was to fire our friend and *Tom Joyner Morning Show* commentator Tavis Smiley, I was upset.

It seemed to me that since there was already a shortage of good programs that served the community on BET, the last thing Mel Karmazin needed to do was to cut any new or political programming. When I spoke to Mel Karmazin about his responsibility to his African American audience, Bob Johnson went off! He called me and told me that HE was the one who made the decision to fire Tavis and the white man had nothing to do with it. He told me that he was still THE MAN making all the decisions at BET, and that I owed him and Mel Karmazin a public apology. Okay, that did it! It was time for me to voice my opinion on the air, and I did. Mel Karmazin might not have known how important shows like Tavis's were to black audiences, but Bob Johnson surely did, and if he really did have his new boss's ear the way he claimed he did, it was pretty sorry for him not to fight, not only for Tavis's show but also for better programming all around.

As a deejay, I have a rule: "Never diss a hardworking brother on the air." After several days of breaking my rule, I agreed to give Bob Johnson time on the *Morning Show* to tell his side of the story. But the more I thought about it, the more I decided against it, because it was one thing to be a stand-up guy and take responsibility for your actions, but it was another thing to be fearful of making your new boss angry, and to be trying to prove that you could protect him from the angry black people (which I believed was Bob Johnson's plan). So when he phoned in at the appointed time, I told him I'd changed my mind and I wouldn't be interviewing him after all. He was understandably angry, and, in retrospect, I should have kept my agreement with him. I should have let him have his say and trusted our audience to be able to decide whether he was on the up and up. So, Bob, if you're reading this, sorry, man.

A lot of people mistakenly thought the whole "battle" between Bob Johnson and me was because Tavis lost his job, which would have been a ridiculous battle, since Tavis had about one hundred other good job offers before, during, and after his stint on BET.

I don't publicly criticize black people on my show mainly because I just believe that there are so many people constantly tearing black people down, there's no reason for me to pile on too. Unless they've committed a heinous crime or done something so ignorant that it can't be ignored, I'll usually give our brothers and sisters the benefit of the doubt . . . on the air. If you lived in a society where you'd seen and heard of black people being jailed and even lynched for things they were accused of but had never been proven guilty of, you too would learn not to be so anxious to point fingers at other people. You also learn to pray for a whole bunch of people you've never met.

I'm not sure how it is for any other race, but for black people every time a crime big enough to make the news is committed, a collective prayer is being made to the heavens: "Lord, please don't let it be a black person." We pray, not because we are personally connected to the criminals—in most cases they are people whose paths will never cross ours. We pray because, real or imagined, we believe that there is guilt by association— they are black and so are we. We pray also because, when watching mainstream media, we are underrepresented as a whole. When we do appear in a news story it is more often than not in a negative light. Our fear is that even though we realize there are more black people who are not committing crimes than those who are, the general public who knows us only by what it sees on the news is not getting that message. And as black people become more successful and have less contact with our old neighborhoods, we sometimes start to have an "Action News" camera view of our people too.

That's why I was so anxious to launch our online news service BlackAmericaWeb.com. Our news service is an honest look at news from a black perspective. When our editors and reporters cover news, sports, features, the entire gamut, they ask questions that are rarely asked by mainstream media. A national study showed that more women were serving in the nation's prisons than ever before, but the study failed to break that number down by race. Our audience hears a story like that and wonders how many of those female inmates are black. BlackAmericaWeb.com was the only news source that broke it down. In fact, when I ask any of my staff to "break it down for me," they know exactly what I mean: "Tell me what it means to and for black people." If you're like me, let's stand together and find ways to continue to do what mainstream America will never do: make black America a priority. It's a black thang.

chapter five

"Take Me to the Next Phase, Baby"

Wherever you live today – I
don't care where it is – isn't
enough. There's more out
there to see and do and
everyone should find a way to
experience life somewhere
else, even if it's just for a
weekend or for even a day.

I CAN'T keep doing the same old thing, the same old way. That may be why I was never a great student. I got bored quickly with the routine of sitting in a classroom listening to someone else talk. I could never keep my mind focused on one thing. Maybe I suffered from ADD, except it hadn't been invented yet. Back then the technical term for my problem was "scatterbrained." So, while the teacher might have been talking about one thing, my mind was on something completely different—like how to get out of Tuskegee.

It's easy for me now to look back and see the benefits of growing up in a nurturing, hustling, bustling black community filled with positive role models, but as a kid that little town felt confining and I needed to escape to somewhere bigger and better. Some place that had more to offer. Some place where I could be free. Some place far, far away . . . like Atlanta. Back then, even before it became known as the black mecca, there was something about Atlanta that beckoned to people in small towns in the South and I was one of those people.

As a kid, I would go to Atlanta with my parents when they wanted to do some serious shopping, that is, shopping for anything other than groceries and household items. There was no place near Tuskegee that came close to offering the variety of stores and shops that existed in Atlanta. So when it was time to purchase clothes or furniture, we headed east.

One of the things I remember most was a department store called Rich's. It just blew me away. It had something that none of the stores in my town had—a husky section! A whole area designated for clothes to fit fat kids like me! It was a beautiful thing.

Atlanta had another thing that caught my eye, well actually my ear, early on: black radio. I can still hear the announcer broadcasting from "the Black and Beautiful Citizens Trust Bank Building." There were no black radio stations in our town back then and the Atlanta station always made me aware of what we were missing. The radio station itself wasn't black-owned but the Citizens Trust Bank Building was. And the on-air talent was black, including Hank Span, the smoothest deejay I had ever heard. He was so cool that when he left the radio station in Atlanta, he went to New York City!

I can still remember how impressed I was with Hank's style and technique. He talked to the records and records would talk back. He had no on-air crew like I have with Sybil, J, Myra, and Ms. Dupre. Instead, he would use recorded voices of people. They didn't say much, just one-liners like "Yeah!" and "That's right!" It might seem corny now, but it was the bomb back in the day. With a "cart machine" full of little comments, he created a whole on-air aura of having people in the studio with him. It was ingenious but probably not as much fun as having a group of people to fool around with while the commercials are playing. Our listeners don't realize this, but on the *Tom Joyner Morning Show* the most fun is had when the commercials are running. That's when we come up with some of the funny material that you hear during the show. It starts off raw, unedited, and off-the-cuff and most of the time we have to clean it up a lot before you get to hear it. I'm considering making recordings of those moments, and calling it the *Tom Joyner Morning Show "Uncut."*

Even though Atlanta was where I decided I would eventually end up, my mind was open to all kinds of different places: the state of Washington, Canada, Hawaii, it didn't really matter. Some of these places I'd read about or seen on television and they appealed to me because they were far away and I figured there would be no way my daddy could make me cut the grass.

But the real reason that I wanted to get out of Tuskegee was because I already had been out of Tuskegee: Thanks to my parents, we had traveled a bit when my brother and I were kids. Aside from the visits to the "country" in southern Alabama and Nashville where my mama's family lived, and parts of Florida, where my daddy's people were from, we took trips to Washington, DC, and to the New York State Fair, and one very memorable and, for me, life-changing vacation to Cuba.

The whole trip to Cuba affected me powerfully, in a way that few things have since. It all began with our arrival in Miami. Although I had been to cities and towns in Florida like Plant City, Tallahassee, and Tampa, none of them compared to the colors I saw, the smells I smelled, and the electricity I felt in Miami. My family and I stayed at a nice black-owned motel with swimming pools and movie stars (I didn't actually see any movie stars but there could have been). Then it got even better in Cuba. The first thing I noticed was the clear blue water in place of the muddy waters of Alabama I was accustomed to. Cuba was simply breathtaking. From that point on I have been in love with the Caribbean and beaches. I was seven years old.

My daddy says on our way back to Tuskegee we stopped in Montgomery and I did something that made my family very nervous. In H. L. Green's I walked up to the "white" lunch counter and struck up a conversation with the white waitresses. I began telling them about our trip to Cuba and I just couldn't stop talking. Being a young kid, I hadn't actually known that much about racism yet. I knew it existed, I'd heard about it, but I had never been the victim of it as far as I knew. So, I talked on. I had to tell these white people what I had experienced, not because they were white, but because they were there—a captive audience. I told them what I had seen and what I felt. And even though I knew I couldn't order any food from that "white" lunch counter, I knew that no one could stop me from talking about what I had seen and done in Cuba. So I held court right there and they all listened to me until I was through.

SEEING ANOTHER part of the world made me yearn for more, and if I hadn't gone on that trip I sometimes wonder how differently my life might have turned out. You never know how something a young child is exposed to can change that child's life. Seeing people living well and living some place beautiful made me want to be surrounded by beauty. I don't know what effect it had on my older brother. I never asked him. But even though he spent the majority of his existence in Alabama, the very place that I left as soon as I could, he and his wife and kids live a very good life and have traveled all across the United States and Europe. He is the owner of more than twenty McDonald's franchises in the Jackson, Mississippi, area and works as hard as I do.

Children need to be exposed to things that will expand their minds. They need to see people doing different things in different places, and they need to see such things firsthand, not on television or at the movies or on the Internet. Wherever you live today—I don't care where it is—isn't eough. There's more out there to see and do and everyone should find a way to experience life somewhere else, even if it's just for a weekend or for even a day.

Whenever I tell people about our vacation to Cuba they ask me whether my parents were rich. Far from it. No. I take that back. They were rich—rich in knowledge and rich in desire to show their children as much of the world as they could. Everyone has that capability. They made a plan, saved their money, and took us on vacations. Not every year; in fact, we didn't do it that often. But it was the quality and not the quantity that made the difference. My parents had a curiosity about the world, so the two of them saved and went on trips overseas to France, Italy, and Russia. And in my community that wasn't a big deal. People were always doing stuff like that because they found a way.

Our neighbors the Childs had a different hunger for adventure than my parents did. They bought a camper, hitched it to the back of a truck, and traveled west to places like Utah and the Grand Canyon. All around us, people who, like my parents, had come to Tuskegee from somewhere else made up their minds that while Tuskegee was a great place to live, it wasn't enough.

Through the years since our trip to Cuba, the Caribbean has continued to be part of my life. When my boys were small we took trips to Jamaica, and, years after that, the *Tom Joyner Morning Show* was born in Montego Bay when I took my new staff of on-air people, producers, and writers to a Jamaican villa for a week to hash out the content of the program.

The annual Fantastic Voyage Cruise that raises money to send kids to black colleges sails to Caribbean ports, and when thousands of black people converge on the islands I know some of them must feel the way I felt the first time I saw Cuba.

We all have to make choices in our life. Not the same choices, but choices nevertheless. Practically everyone I grew up with has left our hometown of Tuskegee, yet, thankfully, a part of Tuskegee has never left us—the part that realized that you never have to settle for what's in front of you. That anything you want to do is worth a try.

When Lionel Richie and I were little boys there was nothing about us that could have made you believe that we would be a success at much of anything. We weren't smart, we weren't cool, we weren't popular. Our identity was linked to people in our lives—I was Albert Joyner's younger brother. Lionel was the schoolteacher Mrs. Richie's son. My brother, Albert, was smarter, athletic, and outgoing. Mrs. Richie was one of the best teachers in our town. But even though we spent most of our youth growing up in the shadow of these two people, we had the guts and the gumption to think we could live out our dream to become entertainers. The hometown people were amazed when they saw shy Lionel out front as lead singer of the Commodores, not to mention his ability to write hit after hit song for the group and for himself when he went solo. I will always believe our success is linked more to our willingness to work hard, and to our refusal to quit trying.

ATLANTA WAS a seven-hour bus ride from Tuskegee and a seven-hour car ride if you followed the bus in a car like my friends did until we figured out a quicker route that knocked the ride down to an hour and fifteen minutes. The longer route was actually better because there was more time to listen to AM radio.

One choice I make daily is whether to be ordinary or extraordinary. Do I want to merely get by or do I want to make a mark? Do I want to settle for what I'm doing or do I want to take it to the next phase? I choose to move forward every chance that I get. Being a local deejay wasn't enough. Being a syndicated deejay on a handful of stations wasn't enough.

If you're not the smartest, the fastest, or the richest, which most of us aren't, you can still be the best if you simply find a way to do things better. For me, better is almost always bigger. When I find an idea or formula that works I keep expanding it. Some of the very ideas that worked when I was deejay at radio station WJPC in Chicago in the '70s are working today on the *Tom Joyner Morning Show.* They've just been revamped and inflated. We didn't have the budget back then to give $1,000 to a deserving mom or dad weekly like we do now. Nor could we afford to grant someone's Christmas wish every Wednesday by providing things like computers, hearing aids, fences, speech therapy, and spa weekends for worn-out sistas like we do now. A thousand dollars to the tenth caller every hour five days a week? Forget about it. But we did try to make a difference by meeting the needs of the community in some creative ways. At WJPC we provided gasoline for 50¢ a gallon when prices had skyrocketed to 90¢ and sometimes even $1 a gallon. (The good old days, right?) It's not such a unique pro-motion now, but thirty years ago it was new and gained lots of free publicity for me and the station. WJPC was owned by my mentor John H. Johnson, and he was pleased with the idea of doing good in the hood while improving the ratings at the same time. Oh what a concept!

At one point, we started selling $25 worth of groceries for $5 on a first-come-first-served basis. The bag included stuff like meat, cereal, bread, and eggs. Once I got on this kick of convincing people who had a lot to share with people who didn't have as much, I couldn't stop. Independence Bank was a black-owned institution in Chicago, where Johnson Publish-ing had an account. I made a deal with them and started sell-ing money at 50 percent off at the drive-thru window. I'd sell you a $10 bill for $5, a $20 bill for $10, etc. Paying listeners' bills was another promotion I launched at WJPC. My primary job was to entertain our audience but it is not easy to be entertained when the bills are piling up and there is no relief in sight. So I found a way to make it happen and take it to the next phase. These promotions we introduced at WJPC wouldn't have been possible without Mr. Johnson's willingness to invest in his audience. When we sold food and money at discount prices, we used the radio station's money to make the difference.

There are always companies and corporations that are willing to donate their products and services. You just have to know whom to ask.

Not long after we went on the air in New York back in 2001, terrorists bombed the World Trade Center on September 11. Thousands were killed and many of their families were left in need. We found a group of black families that needed our help. Instead of sending money to them we delivered it to their homes in person. For days and weeks everyone in the world witnessed the devastation of 9/11 on the news. But entering the homes of mothers and fathers, husbands and wives who had lost their loved ones was something I will never forget.

The *Tom Joyner Morning Show,* though it's syndicated in more than 120 markets, is really just a "local" radio show that's been taken to the next phase. A bigger audience, bigger guests, bigger promotions. Bigger dreams. We try to do on a larger scale what the AM soul stations did during the civil rights movement. Familiarity, compassion, news and information, some laughs, and music you want to hear.

Just like I can tell you I decided I wanted to have a better life after visiting Cuba at the age of seven, I can tell you when I decided I wanted a syndicated radio show, live concert performances, a cruise, and a university. I want all of these things because I want the *Tom Joyner Morning Show* to always be more than average. I want it to be *the* source of entertainment, information, and empowerment for African Americans and I want to make the lives of black people better. As I work toward making the show bigger and better, I employ more people, reach out to more people, and get more hugs. That's partly why I keep stepping it up, but it's mostly because, just like back in grade school, I still can't sit still. If you were always one of those kids who had to keep moving, you're probably still the same way now, so channel your energy into moving ahead. Never be content with staying in one place. Take it to the next phase, baby!

chapter six

"If You Can't Be with the One You Love, Love the One You're With"

The world is not standing still, and if you are, you're going to be left behind.

SOMETIMES AFTER taking it to the next phase, we realize it's time to take a detour. On our journey to success it's inevitable that we'll run into detours and setbacks that we can't control. In other words, we're going to get fired, we're going to quit, we're going to break up, we're going to relocate, we're going to get put out, we're going to fail, and we're going to lose our hair. Or, maybe it's just me.

In my twenty-three years on this earth (yes, I said twenty-three!), I have been through a lot and the one thing I know for sure is, whether you fail or succeed, you don't need to spend too much time reflecting on either. Failure is part of life, and once you've given something your best shot and it still isn't working, you need to move on. I think most people realize that. What most people don't realize is you need to do the same thing when you have successes. If you're spending lots of time celebrating one success, you're losing focus on other opportunities you could and should be pursuing. Always keep your eye on the prize ahead, not the one you've already seized.

When you're going to celebrate a victory, don't start celebrating too soon. Have you ever watched a football player ten yards out from the end zone raising the ball in the air to celebrate his anticipated touchdown? An opponent comes out of nowhere and snatches the ball right out of his hands? No matter how successful you are, or think you are, there's always someone out there who can rob you of your moment, especially if you're partying instead of preparing for what's up ahead.

If you're going to be a success in life, you need to keep doing whatever it was that got you that victory and a whole lot more. Keep moving forward and don't look back. The surest way to lose a footrace is to keep looking back at your opponents. If you keep your eye on the finish line, you're more likely to get there ahead of the pack. People who have achieved success in any area—business, entertainment, education, you name it—don't quit striving after one achievement. They're like good athletes. They don't quit after one win. They're up early the next morning practicing or training just as hard as they did the day before. The only time you should be looking back is to grab the hand of someone who may be following in your footsteps.

I like to box. One of the most painful lessons I learned in the ring was to keep swinging after I landed a good punch. I'd be so proud and surprised when I'd hit my opponent, I would pause, and the next thing I knew—bam!—he had swung at me. That's the way it is in life too. If you land a good punch, don't stop fighting. If you do, you'll get knocked out. If you don't believe me, ask Roy Jones Jr.

Always define your goals and keep reminding yourself of why you're striving for them. Make sure you're not working hard purely for money or recognition. Don't get me wrong, there's nothing wrong with desiring fame and fortune, but it needs to go deeper than that. You have to have a love for what you're doing. If you don't, it's too easy to throw in the towel too soon and be left with nothing to work toward. If you're going to stay on top, something other than money has got to motivate you. I've been blessed to have a very successful career in radio and have made a lot of money. But if I were only motivated by money, I would have been finished years ago when my "Turntable Brother" Doug Banks and I became the first deejays in the history of Chicago radio to earn $1 million a year.

It was contract negotiation time back in the '80s at radio station WGCI and Doug and I decided to bargain with management as a package. If each of us weren't going to make $1 million, both of us were going to quit. Were we each worth $1 million? Absolutely! And we were able to prove it. Back then white deejays in Chicago were making $750,000 with ratings not nearly as high as ours. Doug was making $300,000, and even though no radio station anywhere else in the country or in the world was going to pay him more than that, he was ready to fight for what he was worth.

I wasn't thinking about fighting at the time, but he was my brother and Doug and I knew that we put the "G" and the "C" in WGCI. Without us the station would suffer a huge financial loss.

Be prepared to show your boss why you're an asset to the company and have a plan for what you contribute in the future BEFORE you demand a raise. Instead of telling your boss why you need more money, tell your boss why you deserve it. Or, be ready to make a really big threat that you can back up. We got an agent to convince the bosses at WGCI that if they didn't pay us each $750,000 apiece, we would go to the competition and beat them. There was one small glitch. We had no offers from the competition, but we got friend Barry Mayo, who had just purchased radio station WBMX in Chicago, to put on paper that he would pay us $1 million apiece to come work for him and we showed that offer to our boss, Marv Dyson. He didn't know whether it was a bluff or not, and he never found out for sure what happened . . . until now. Doug and I became millionaires. And just like the people who were handed out the money on *The Millionaire* we blew a whole lot of it!

Change is good, even when things are going perfectly well. Just because you're succeeding, don't be afraid to go in another direction and try something new. You'll get a lot of criticism because most people get to a certain place in life and become comfortable, and they expect you to do the same. If you are working at a job right now that you've had for years, nothing will shake your loved ones up more than for you to announce that you're quitting to pursue something else. "What!!!?" "You're gonna quit your *good* job and do *what?*!!!" "Have you lost your mind?" I can't tell you how many times these questions have been posed to me. Thankfully, in most cases, I ignored them and moved ahead.

A huge part of being successful is knowing when to change lanes. When you're on the road and you're really trying to get somewhere, eventually you need to get out of the lane you're in. There are several ways to do it. You can jump out too soon without checking your mirror. You can turn your signal on way too early and be afraid to get over. You can wait until the person next to you waves you over and gives you permission. Or you can put your signal on at the right moment and jump in there before the rest of the cars can do anything about it. That's me. Whenever I made a major career or personal change in my life it took planning, it took timing, it took aggressiveness, and it took risk. Or . . . I had just gotten fired!

I made a big lane change when I took the syndication deal at ABC Radio Networks. Once again, I had decided to retire from radio, or at least slow down a whole lot. I had been flying back and forth from Dallas to Chicago daily for eight years, logging more than seven million miles on American Airlines, and that had finally ended. By the way, in case you're wondering, all I got from American Airlines was the leather first-class seats I'd sat in and lot of frequent flier miles. Some thanks, although the seats do seem to impress people when they visit our broadcast studio in Dallas. But I was sick and tired of flying every day and so was my family.

I got a contract with CBS to do a syndicated weekend countdown show called *On the Move* and I planned to kick back and become the black Casey Kasem. He had made millions with his national show and I figured I could put together a similar format with R&B hits and comedy bits. The sketches, by the way, were produced in Los Angeles with L.A. comics and writers that included Brad Sanders, Myra J., Tommy Davidson, Guy Torrie, Daryl Singleton, Martin Lawrence, Greg Eagleton, Doug Starks, Rusty Condiff, who went on to write a major film and become a staff writer for Dave Chappelle's hit show, and Mary Boyce, who would later become my head writer and who is my collaborator on this book. Others like Roxanne Reese, Jedda Jones (Ms. Dupre), and Buddy Lewis later became regular characters on our daily radio soap opera, *It's Your World*. In fact, most of the people who work with me today I've worked with in some capacity for nearly twenty years.

The deal with CBS was made and my life had become a whole lot less complicated. *On the Move* took off and was going well. It was sort of like the calm before the storm. Everything was fine until I got a phone call from ABC Radio Networks that turned everything upside down. The company was in the midst of expanding its urban format and it wanted that expansion to include me. The offer to go national was an offer I just could not refuse. It would take me to a place where I never imagined I'd be. Well, not really. I had imagined the whole thing and even discussed it with one of the corporate guys at ABC once before. But when it was presented back to me as though it was their own idea, I let them have it. Sometimes you need to know when to shut up. What difference did it make whose idea it was anyway? The main thing was, I had the opportunity to do something no black man had ever done before. No, not date Whoopi! Host a nationally syndicated radio program.

I knew if I took this deal at this point in my life, I would have to give it all that I had. I knew that an offer like this wouldn't come around again and I knew if I failed . . . I'd have nowhere to go in radio but down. That was a scary thought because I had never taken a step backward in my entire career. I had stood still for a while and I had made some lateral moves, but mostly I had moved forward my whole life. Did I want to risk my winning record of moving to the top, blow my sure thing at CBS and my syndicated countdown show, gamble it all away for a history-making leap into the unknown? Hell yeah! It was a massive step in my professional life and it was massive personally too, because it was at this point that my marriage to my sons' mother, Dora, ended.

In a sense, I married the *Tom Joyner Morning Show.* I had to create something brand-new from the ground up that was completely different from anything I had done before. It couldn't be a *Dallas* show that was heard all over the country. It had to feel local to every market it was heard in. I had to take what had been successful in the past and "step it up." But before I could do anything, I had to sever my ties with CBS. It was painful—I'm sure more for them than for me—and I felt bad when I had to tell the people who offered me what was, then, a deal of a lifetime, that I had gotten a better deal from their competition.

When you change lanes, sometimes people you care about get hurt emotionally and financially. A whole team of people were put in place to produce *On the Move,* and all of a sudden, because of my good fortune, they were left in the lurch. But I was "on the move" literally, and said good-bye to CBS for good. I bought out my contract, and CBS took back the name of the weekend show. I had decided to continue with the countdown show at ABC and when I told Brad Sanders we had to change the name of *On The Move* he didn't miss a beat. *Movin' On,* he said. Perfect.

Getting the new syndicated radio show where I wanted it was foremost on my mind and I had my team from back in the day to help me do it. For years I had done soap opera updates with Los Angeles writer Brad Sanders as the character named Cla'ence. He would call in daily and tell our listeners what was happening on their favorite soaps. I hired him and Myra J. to create a soap opera for the new *Tom Joyner Morning Show,* and that became "It's Your World." It was our version of the day's most popular soaps and when I heard the first episode I knew we had a winner. Once again, we had come up with something that had never been done on black radio, and it was just one of the things that made the *Tom Joyner Morning Show* unique.

Throughout my life and career I've learned to ignore the four words that are quick to be spoken by people who are willing to give up too easily: "It Can't Be Done." Usually, "It Can't Be Done" simply means it hasn't been done before, and to that I say, good! That means we'll be ahead of the rest.

When we debuted in January 1994, our first guest was Luther Vandross. He brought our audience into his kitchen and cooked breakfast. We had a live band led by Butch Stewart, Uncle Butchie and the Live House. Butch's company writes and produces some of corporate America's most successful commercial jingles and creates all the jingles for the *Morning Show,* like "It's Your World," "Real Fathers, Real Men," "Christmas Wish," and my show's theme, sing it with me ya'll, "Oh, Oh, Oh, It's the Tom Joyner Morning Show."

The world is not standing still, and if you are, you're going to be left behind. If you're surprised to find out that things are changing, it's probably too late for you to do anything about it.

You can either be a catalyst of change or a victim of it. It's your choice. When I decided to change lanes and accept the offer to host the nationally syndicated *Tom Joyner Morning Show,* I knew that radio was changing and I had gone as far as I could in the traditional radio format. I knew this not because I had been talking to Ms. Dupre, our resident psychic, I knew it because I had done my homework. Unless I made a move, my career would be over.

A lot of people didn't see it coming and many of the same guys in the industry who thought I was making a grave mistake now find themselves looking for a shot at syndication—a shot that most of them will never get. They're fifty plus (it's funny how they got older and I remained twenty-three), and they're doing the exact same thing they were doing twenty years ago, if they're lucky. The unlucky ones are out of the business. I wish I could help them all, but I can't.

Sometimes, though, even I can get knocked off guard by change, like the night I attended a Jay-Z/R. Kelly concert in Dallas with some of my Reach Media staff. At no time had the differences and similarities between old school and new school become more clear to me. The arena was 60 percent white and 40 percent black and they were all partying together and caught up in the hype. It wasn't at all the crowd I had expected, because I had been dealing with perception instead of truth. There were a lot of young people there but there were a whole lot of people who were over thirty too. Most, judging by their cars, their outfits, and their ability to pay $75 for a ticket, were doing okay financially in a bad economy. And they all had come to party. This is my demo, I said, checking out the people around me. They were jammin' to songs that made our radio affiliates scream bloody murder when I tried to slip them in.

Then the audience did something that totally amazed me.

As Jay-Z yelled "'N word' what!" "'N word' who!" the inte-
grated crowd chanted those words back to him. There they
were, screaming the "N word," black and white together, and
I thought to myself, *This definitely wasn't what Dr. King had in
mind.* My crew included people whose ages ranged from
twenty-something to nearly forty and when I watched them
during Jay-Z's performance I realized that the younger the
person, the louder the "N word."

For the record, I was a silent observer. I'm just a deejay, but
there's no way in the world a kid like me from Tuskegee who
had marched for civil rights and done everything I knew to do
to uplift black people could be caught raising my fist in the air
shouting the "N word" in the presence of white people. That
night I was the oldest twenty-three-year-old black man in the
world. But mostly I was glad that I hadn't gotten caught up in
the hype.

I don't claim to condone everything the hip-hop culture
produces, but I also think there are some extremely positive as-
pects to it. Most people who announce that hip-hop is a negative, misogynistic promoter of drugs and violence are
repeating what they've heard someone else say. Rarely is any
other category of music painted with such a broad stroke.
Take rock music, for example. For every negative rap or hip-
hop lyric, you could find a rock lyric that is equally offensive.
Like rock, rap is an artistic expression that speaks to a particular generation. That generation continues to age, and just as
it's common to see rockers who are fifty plus, there is a huge
fan base of hip-hop music who are over forty. I'm constantly
battling with management on our affiliate stations who think
rap is for the thirty and under crowd. My stations need to
"young-up." I love old school but to keep current and to keep
advertisers, we have got to play music that young people like.

After all, we're losing a lot of our old-school artists, literally (Barry White, Rick James, Tyrone Davis).

If you think hip-hop music is the cause of gang violence, or drug use, or the prison population, let's look at it another way. Let's look at the other things that were occurring in this country at the same time hip-hop was born. Like the ultraconservative Reagan administration and the disappearance of government programs designed to help poor children. Gone were after-school programs. Playgrounds were shut down. The money set aside for jobs and job training for inner-city youth dried up along with scholarships and grants earmarked for kids in low-income families. At the same time, material things, designer clothes, and rich lifestyles were glorified in the media like never before. Poverty in America was no longer a circumstance looked at with compassion. Suddenly, it was looked at with hatred and disdain. You could be poor but you sure as hell couldn't look like it.

The most popular television programs of the time were *Dynasty, Dallas*, and *Lifestyles of the Rich and Famous*. No one wanted to be reminded that an underclass existed—not even the underclass itself. How many pairs of designer jeans did you have in the '80s? What size were those jeans? Okay, okay, that's none of my business. Inner-city kids wearing anything but name-brand or designer clothes were ashamed to be seen at school and many parents who couldn't put a dime in a savings account spent nearly $100 a pop on sneakers. If the advertising industry put it out there we spent money on it, and those of us who couldn't earn the money to buy what America was selling found a way to get it anyway.

Poor minorities weren't the only ones who got burned livin' large by any means necessary. Affluent Americans were just as guilty and plenty of them went to federal prisons for getting caught up in the excesses we all began to feel entitled to whether we could afford them or not. Credit card debt went through the roof and it took many of us decades to pay for that high-ticket, high-interest stuff we had to have in the '80s.

America sent a me-first, buy-now-pay-later message to the middle and upper classes and forgot that the poor people were getting the same signals. What happens when you teach a generation of people that their self-worth is determined by the label of clothes they wear, the type of cars they drive, and the amount of gold they flaunt? What happens when you simultaneously take away their access to education and jobs?

Instead of spending so much time blaming hip-hop for all that's wrong with America, let's figure out how to fill the void America left for the hip-hop generation. It's time to dedicate ourselves to making higher education accessible to poor and minority students and showing them its benefits. Someone will always argue that poor kids won't take the time to attend college when they can get rich in a hurry selling drugs. That's another myth. Sure there are a lot of inner-city kids selling drugs but there are just as many working at minimum-wage jobs, enrolled in junior colleges, and enlisted in the military.

Plenty of those kids would and could be enrolled in a four-year university. There are millions of college dropouts whose circumstances have not allowed them to re-enroll in a traditional university and there are others who have never attended college but would like to get the skills needed for advancing in their jobs. Instead of fearing the future and all it brings, we need to be working on ways of being more prepared for all it brings.

In your job, at your school, in your community, in your home, you need to be ready to deal with whatever life brings you. If it means making some changes in your life, don't cry about it. We don't get to choose the life we have but we have a lot of choices in how we'll live it, and since we only live once, why waste time moping around? If you can't have the life you love, love the one you've got. And make it the best you can.

chapter seven

It's Your Name, Do What You Wanna Do

In the end I guess I'm sort of glad to be known simply as Tom Joyner because it pays homage to my daddy and all the other Joyners before him.

HERE'S A tip: If you give your child a name that can fit into the name-game song, he or she will be grateful to you. It should be a name that won't be mispronounced or misspelled very often. Tyquonda is a beautiful name, don't get me wrong, but if you want to find your daughter a personalized license plate for her bike, you might be out of luck.

Because I'm a deejay and talk to hundreds of listeners a month who phone in, I hear many unique names and I'm surprised when a caller seems offended if I don't get the pronunciation right the first time. We get some callers with names that sound like medications and diseases—like Ambiceen and Colestera. Some are combinations of male and female names, like Arthurine and Calvinetta. And then there are the names that are unexplainable, like Tashaniqua, Calamity, and Blenda.

Some names that sound bizarre to us, however, make perfect sense to the parents who chose them, so we shouldn't be too quick to judge. For example, Luther Vandross has always been known to his family as Ronnie, which is short for Ronzoni, his middle name. His mom, Evangelist Mary Ida, told me when she was pregnant with Luther the only thing she could eat that wouldn't make her sick was Ronzoni pasta, so that's all she ate. She vowed that she would name her baby Ronzoni and that's how Luther Ronzoni Vandross got his name. All I can say is thank goodness Mrs. Vandross didn't eat a lot of asparagus.

I've learned a lot about celebrities' names over the years. Frankie Beverly of the group Maze isn't really Frankie at all. He's Howard! He was such a huge fan of the teen sensation Frankie Lymon when he was a kid, he just jacked his name and kept it for himself. Thankfully, he didn't take on the personality flaws of Frankie Lymon, like being married to several women at the same time. Rent the movie.

Stevie Wonder, formerly known as Little Stevie Wonder, is really Steveland Morris. Stevie Wonder may not be such a cool name for, say, an auto mechanic, but for a musical genius with as many Grammys as he has braids in his hair, it's a great name. I'm glad Stevie got to the point where he realized it was time to drop the "Little." Lil' Bow Wow did the same thing. He's now just Bow Wow. But some people still don't get it. Yes, I'm calling you out, Little Richard! Even if you're still little and you're over sixty, stop calling yourself "Little." Here that, Lil' Kim? You've got about thirty years!

The same thing goes for you Juniors out there. Jesse Jackson Jr., for example, has a reason for continuing to use "Jr." after his name because his father is still out there fighting the good fight. Same thing with actor Cuba Gooding Jr. His father is still in the music business as lead singer of the R&B group the Main Ingredient and it's possible that someone could get confused if Cuba dropped the Jr.

Roy Jones Jr., however, is iffy. Even though his dad is still around, we know he's not going to be boxing anytime soon. So when Roy Jones Jr. is about to go up against an opponent in the ring, I think just plain old Roy Jones is enough.

But then take someone like the late actor Douglas Fairbanks Jr. He was like two hundred years old when he died. He could have dropped the Jr. about seventy-five years ago and I think he would have been fine.

Speaking of stars, they're also guilty of being, let's just say, *very creative* when it comes to naming their children. Erykah Badu named her two children Seven and Puma. Jermaine Jackson named his youngest son Jermajesty. George Foreman named all five of his sons after him, George.

There are some names that sort of bring certain things to mind. Rightly or wrongly, they just do. For example, a girl named Toni or Jackie is kind of fast, at least in my mind. If a caller says her name is Ethel or Fannie, I think of an old auntie, and no matter how fine she tells me she is, I won't believe her. Amy and Becky are white girls. Jerome and Tyrone are brothas. And Candy, Nikki, and Angie may, let's see, how can I say this, have poles in their futures, as in "Gentlemen, give it up for Nikki! Come on and Git it, Git it, Git it, Git it!"

My name is simply Tom, which is an okay name for most professions, but it's not the best name for a deejay. I'd always wished I had come up with a cool deejay name when I first started out in radio. I often thought of changing it to something else over the years, but every cool name I heard already belonged to another deejay. There was "BBD the Banana," "The Voice," "Herb Kent the Cool Gent," and one I surely should have thought of—"Thomas the Promise." There was already a "Bama Burner," so I couldn't use that name either. My biggest problem was that I was always trying to think of something to rhyme with "Tuskegee." Even Jesse Jackson would have a tough time with that.

When hip-hop and rap came out, those artists came up with some cool names that I wish I'd thought of too, like Sir Mix-A-Lot, Spinderella, and Terminator X of Public Enemy. LL Cool J's deejay is "the Cut Creator." Those are great deejay names!

But rappers have some problematic names too. I mean, I understand gangsta rappers' efforts to sound hard, but some of those names rarely help them if they should happen to appear somewhere like, say for instance, court! C-Murder, for example, was up on, uh, *murder* charges a few years ago. Mack-10, who is the ex-boyfriend of TLC member T-Boz, was accused of threatening her life. Mack-10, by the way, is the name of an automatic weapon . . .

I finally came up with the Hardest Working Man in Radio for my handle. In a way it was a salute to one of my favorite performers of all time, the Godfather of Soul, James Brown, who was always introduced as the Hardest Working Man in Show Business. I had seen Soul Brother Number One perform and he always gave it everything he had. I liked that, and even though I may not have been the best at what I did, I always did my best and gave it my all. If I can point to one thing that has allowed me to do what I do as long as I have, hard work would be it.

Somewhere along the way I picked up the nickname "the Fly Jock." While I was working at WGCI in Chicago, a production guy named Richard Peguee created a jingle about me flying back and forth daily from Dallas to Chicago to do the morning and afternoon time slots. He called me "the Fly Jock" and it stuck, although I must admit I had my doubts about the name when someone sent me a picture of a jockstrap with a fly on it.

In the end I guess I'm sort of glad to be known simply as Tom Joyner because it pays homage to my daddy and all the other Joyners before him. I wonder if celebrities who choose to be known by only their first names realize how that must make their families feel. Brandy, Monica, Jaheim, Usher, Kem—they all have family members who have a heck of a time trying to convince their fellow employees down at the post office that they're related to the one-name person singing on the radio. The way I look at it, no matter how big a star you become, someone in your family took you to music lessons,

voice lessons, dance lessons, paid for your first Jheri curl, or
something! Give them the satisfaction of seeing their last
name in lights along with yours.

Aside from its not being the coolest deejay name in the
world, the name "Tom" was also a potential problem for me
when I became an uncle. The last thing in the world I ever
wanted to be known as was Uncle Tom. So, to Allison,
Danielle, and Bubba (Albert Jr.), I'm known as Uncle Happenin'. The only thing about giving yourself a name like
Uncle Happenin' is you have got to make certain that you are
exactly that . . . Happenin' at all times. It hasn't been easy, but
I think I've lived up to it so far. This mainly entails getting the
kids the coolest stuff before their father, my brother, Albert,
has had a chance to get it, or better yet, getting them stuff he
told them they couldn't have in the first place. My favorite
thing when they were really small was to tell them I gave
Santa Claus the money to buy them their Christmas presents!
Now that's Happenin'!

Most of the men in my family were named after grandparents and uncles. It's a way of forever being connected to your
ancestors and it gives you a sense of who you are. I'm thankful,
though, that my dad, Hercules, didn't name me or my brother
after him. In other words, if you have a messed-up first name,
don't keep it going. I'm sure my daddy got enough whippings
for being named Hercules to last a lifetime and he decided that
was not a legacy he wanted to pass down. My father's father
was named Oscar and he had a brother named Albert. My
brother, who was the firstborn, was named Albert, and he has
a son Albert Jr. My two sons are Thomas Elliot Jr. and Oscar
Albert. We may not be very original in the Joyner family, but
we're consistent. If you name your children after their ancestors, you give them a connection to their roots. And if you
name them after someone who's dead, you pretty much know

what kind of legacy that person left behind. You don't have to worry that you could be naming your child after someone who eventually becomes an armed felon. It's just the safest route, in my opinion. That's why federal buildings and schools are normally named after dead people. It's a good policy, because you just never know. Can you imagine if someone had decided to name a high school after O. J. Simpson fifteen years ago?

I know I spent a lot of time denouncing the whole junior theory, and I stand by my earlier remarks. You see I never intended to have a junior, but that's the price you pay for not being there when the birth certificate is filled out. I'm sure there are many men out there who have little to say when it comes to officially naming their children, simply because they're not around. And I'm not talking about dads who are absent from their children's lives. I'm talking about dads who may have gone down to the hospital cafeteria to get a bowl of chili when the mother gives the nurse the info. The hospital ought to at least make sure the dad signs off on the name before it becomes official. Anyway, since I didn't get to give my firstborn his first name, I did get a chance to give him his nickname—Killer, after DuPont member Killer Craig. My second son is nicknamed Thriller. If we'd had another child, he would have been called Driller. I'm very big on nicknames because you can get as silly as you want to with them, but still give your kid a sophisticated name that will look good on a résumé or on an office door. For example, Peaches is a cute nickname, but you may not want that to be the name of your primary care physician . . . especially if it's male.

When I was a kid growing up, I had no idea that "Tom Joyner" would become a brand name. When my son Oscar came to work for Reach Media after getting his MBA from Florida A&M, he was very concerned about making clear the differences between Tom Joyner the man and Tom Joyner the brand. He has a hand in everything that has the Tom Joyner name on it: the radio show, the foundation, the cruise, the Sky Shows, the Tom Joyner Family Reunion, and our casual clothing line, Joyner Gear. My name, in a sense, now belongs to all of our employees, radio affiliates, sponsors, and anyone who is connected with any of those entities. Oscar is always looking for ways to associate the name "Tom Joyner" with projects and events that promote a positive brand image.

Being a brand is a big responsibility. If I screw up it's not just me that suffers. The people who work for me and with me will also feel the sting. That means I need to make good and wise choices and be prepared to take the heat for the times when I don't. But really, Tom Joyner the brand shouldn't be that different from Tom Joyner the man. Long before I'd ever heard the term "brand image" I was creating one and so were you. How you treat people, your work ethic, your personal relationships—all are being examined by other people and will be associated with your name. The sooner you realize that, the sooner you have the opportunity to begin thinking about how the choices you make today may come back and smack you and your family upside the head in the future.

Will Smith says his father told him to live his life as though he would someday become the president of the United States. Will says that advice anchored him and helped him to make good decisions. What have you done in your past that would ruin your hopes to be president if the press got a hold of it? Yeah . . . me too. Of course, the question is, no matter how honorably we live our lives, can there ever be a president named Tu'Shon?

I'm not saying only people with common names achieve success. Nothing is further from the truth. Thurgood, Condoleezza, Denzel, and Oprah weren't held back by their unique names. However, studies have shown that those in hir-

ing positions in corporate America routinely prejudge résumés of people with "ethnic"-sounding names. So are we
hurting our kids when we name them after cars, and liquor,
and makers of clothes that we buy knockoff versions of? Do
Lexus, Tequilla, or Chanelle get as many interviews as Lisa,
Tammy, and Cheryl? And what about the new-school babies,
Escalade, Alize', and Encye? What kind of future do they
have?

I happen to be one of those people who believes that everything screwed up or even a little bit off about black people can
be traced back to slavery, and I think the name game is an example. When slaves were stripped away from their families
they eventually lost touch with their heritage and traditions.
When we criticize our people for giving their children made-
up names, we should consider the fact that our ancestors did
the same thing practically out of necessity. Their choice was either to give their children the American name of someone
who brought them nothing but pain and despair or to begin a
fresh tradition by creating a name that was completely unique.
When you think about it, every name was made up at some
point. So maybe those of us who are so judgmental of people
who think outside the box when it comes to naming their kids
ought to just let it go. Who wants his child to have the same
name as every Tom, Dick, and Harry . . . or make that every
Tyrese, Diondre, and Hisani?

Times really are changing. Forty years ago LaKeisha was a
unique name, but if you attend a graduation ceremony at a
black college today, LaKeisha is as common as the name
Sharon or Darlene was back in the day. There are doctors,
teachers, politicians, and, yes, Big Mamas named LaKeisha
today. And of course the spellings will vary, so if you don't
know how to spell it, just ask the LaKeisha. She'll be glad to
tell you. It's no different from going to a white elementary

school and seeing Kristen spelled five different ways by five different little girls: Kristen, Krysten, Christen, Crysten, and Kristyn.

And for you employers out there in corporate America who are tossing résumés in the trash if the names appear to be a little too ethnic, that's as ignorant as judging a person by the color of his skin . . . oh yeah, a lot of you still do that too! All I can say is you are limiting yourselves and missing out on opportunities to meet and possibly hire people who could do wonders for your companies. In the meantime at our company, Reach Media, we'll consider applications from all the LaChandras, D'Amanis, and Travantees out there. And when the next Bill Gates is named Quandrae, I'm just going to sit back and laugh, and pray he'll come to work for us.

chapter eight

"Ain't No Mountain High Enough"

*When you find a cause, a
mission, a project you're
willing to see through to the
end that isn't motivated by
money, you'll get a feeling far
better than anything any
material possession
can bring you.*

IN THE 2004 presidential election, the Reverend Al Sharpton threw his hair, I mean his hat, into the ring and decided to become a candidate on the Democratic ticket. I supported him because he convinced me that he would force both major parties to address issues that were of importance to people of color. For months I listened to him and watched him do and say all the right things, but much of white and black America couldn't hear him because they couldn't get past the perm. A week didn't go by without someone saying to me, "Tom, you know Al Sharpton, you have his ear, tell him to get rid of that perm." I wanted to, because as much as I supported him, I would wake up in a cold sweat picturing him in the White House with half a head of relaxer. But I just couldn't tell him my feelings because I knew the perm, for him, was more than a hairstyle.

Sharpton says that when he was a child, James Brown, "the Godfather of Soul," had a major influence on him. He became a father figure to Rev. Al and had an impact on his life. He wears that perm to pay tribute to a person he loves and respects. The hairstyle may cause him to lose love and respect today, and it certainly caused him to lose some votes, but as badly as he wanted to become the Democratic nominee for president, he had made a decision years ago to wear that perm and that's what he did. He was committed.

There ought to be at least one thing in your life that you're completely committed to, that you're willing to stand by through thick and thin, not because it's always perfect, not because it's always right, not because it always benefits you, but because you've made up your mind and decided in your heart that you'll be there. It might be your church, it might be your marriage, it might be your sorority, it might be your hairstyle. One of the beautiful things about a commitment is that it isn't always fifty-fifty. That means sometimes you're giving more, sometimes you're giving less, sometimes you're taking more, and sometimes you're taking less. Sometimes you're doing all the giving, sometimes you're doing all the taking, and nobody's mad about it.

The whole premise of the Historically Black Colleges and Universities, from their inception in the 1800s, was to give "colored" students a place to receive "separate but equal" education after high school so they could become skilled, productive citizens in a mostly separate and mostly unequal society. It was a system committed to educating African American high school graduates when no one else would or could. The system has graduated such people as Martin Luther King Jr., Ed Bradley, Walter Payton, Debbie Allen, Jesse Jackson, Alex Haley, George Washington Carver, George Curry, Charlie Wilson, Spike Lee, Tim Reid, and Barbara Jordan, to name just a few.

Historically Black Colleges and Universities have probably given more to the students who attended them than the students ever could repay. But since I can't speak for every student who attended an HBCU, I'll speak for myself. Aside from the basic education I received in the five years it took me to earn my bachelor of science degree—and, yes, I said five years—I gained a sense of pride, a sense of confidence, a sense of community, and a sense of history from the Tuskegee Institute. I am the poster child of what an HBCU can do for a person who struggled to get a C-. If you're a C student or below and you ever get discouraged about your future, think of me and realize that you can make it! You can be proud. You can be confident. You can care about your community. You can care about your history.

Bill Cosby and his wife, Camille, are huge supporters of Historically Black Colleges and Universities. Aside from the monetary gifts they have given to various schools, Mr. Cosby speaks about the importance of supporting the institutions with passion, and believes wholeheartedly in what they can do for black children. His late son, Ennis, was an HBCU graduate and Mr. Cosby loves to tell personal stories of how his son's teaching career was guided by caring professors.

Throughout his television series *The Cosby Show*, he presented story lines that showed black colleges in a positive way and introduced the concept of attending a black college to youth who may never have considered it. He took it a step further with a *Cosby* spin-off series, *A Different World*, a fictionalized view of life on an HBCU campus. For some, it was the first glimpse of a black college and I've heard young people say that it influenced their decision to attend one. Since I, like many born and raised in the South, knew black colleges as part of my heritage, it was amazing to me to discover that there were actually black people out there who weren't familiar with HBCUs. My grandparents on both sides, my parents, my older brother, my two sons, and niece are all graduates of Historically Black Colleges and Universities. When my sons Thomas and Oscar were ready to consider colleges, I told them they could go anywhere they wanted to go, as long as it was an HBCU.

So you see, it wasn't by coincidence that my family members all attended HBCUs, it was by commitment. I meet parents all the time who proudly tell me that they are HBCU grads with two, sometimes three children currently enrolled in three different black colleges. They realize that when you're committed to something, you find a way to make it work and you find the best in what you've committed to. There will always be something else that comes along that can offer something different and sometimes even something more appealing, but if you're honorable and loyal, you honor the commitment that you've made.

Up until 1954 when the U.S. Supreme Court struck down the policy of "separate but equal" schools, for most black Americans, black colleges were the only game in town. After desegregation, some African Americans who could afford them or had the grades began to attend predominantly white schools. And later, as it became financially lucrative to have blacks enrolled, mainstream institutions began to recruit black students, often for their athletic ability.

Many blacks continued to go to black colleges because they didn't have the finances or the credentials to attend mainstream colleges. But many who could have gone to white colleges went to black colleges out of commitment and because they realized these institutions had something great to offer. Statistics have shown that black students who attend HBCUs are more likely to graduate than students who attend mainstream institutions. Not only that, but *Fortune* 500 companies are more likely to hire students who have graduated from HBCUs than they are to hire black kids from mainstream colleges.

I've always believed we perform better when we're expected to perform well. At HBCUs almost everyone is either expecting students to succeed or hoping and praying really hard that they will, and when I talk about succeeding, I'm talking about graduating. It's no secret that a large number of black students attend junior and mainstream four-year colleges on athletic scholarships where the emphasis is placed on doing whatever it takes to make and remain on the team. The kinds of extra help and attention kids on athletic scholarships receive at these schools often help sustain them just long enough to make sure they're able to play. A lot of kids need this kind of support whether they're ballers or not. It's no wonder that a lot of black kids think becoming a pro athlete is their only ticket to financial independence or at least to buying mama a new house. For some, it's the only time they ever see themselves or their peers being rewarded and even cheered for.

Are your children getting the same praise for a good grade on a book report as they get when they sink a basket at a game? If they aren't, they should. How much time does your kid spend practicing for his sports team compared to the time he spends studying for a math test? Rev. Jesse Jackson says we excel in sports because we practice. When they commit an equal amount of time to academics our kids excel in classwork too. Sometimes it's harder to motivate them toward schoolwork since it isn't common to see a black member of a championship spelling bee team showing off his mansion and eight-car garage on *Cribs*.

Athletes who attend Historically Black Colleges and Universities probably won't get as much national attention as they would if they attended a Pac 10 university, nor will they be as likely to be drafted by a professional team. So, if you think the purpose of college is to serve as a farm for breeding pros, an HBCU probably shouldn't be your first choice. If you believe, like I do, that college is a place to learn and develop and work toward a goal of completion, then I ask you to consider an HBCU. It's never too late to begin a family tradition!

Being in a nurturing environment, kids who attend HBCUs develop a sense of themselves, a sense of their heritage, and a heck of a good spades game. I would love to see a national card game challenge between any HBCU and a mainstream university graduate. Don't get me wrong, I'd never propose that you send your child to an HBCU based on a school's record for spades victories, but I do think things like spades, bid whist, and dominoes or anything else that rounds out a student's academic experience is very positive.

More than anything, college teaches you about life—and spades is a great metaphor for living. The game involves choosing a partner, trusting that partner, working together as a team, taking risks, dealing with the consequences when you come up short, and talking a whole lot of trash when you're victorious. You say that talking trash when you win is poor sportsmanship? Maybe, but remember, we're talking about real life. Now, when you talk trash in the game of spades or anything else, there's a chance that you'll get a "behind whip-pin'" if you go too far. The sooner you learn this lesson the better. Spades often incorporates the "rise and fly" rule. That means if you and your partner lose a hand, you have to get up and give the next team your seats. Typically you're laughed at and talked about as you leave. Being able to walk away from a humiliating situation with any sense of dignity is a tool that can be utilized in real life over and over. Maybe that's why I've been able to get fired and move on without having thoughts of suicide or shooting up the place. Having thirty people point at me while yelling, "I thought you could play," and a partner looking at me like I was crazy for bidding eight when I actually was holding two, possibly three, taught me never to crumble in the face of adversity—at least not while anyone was looking.

There's an old saying: "You need to dance with the one that brung you." And that's what we need to do. Black colleges were here for us when nothing else was. They "brung" us a long way and the least we can do is continue to support them, even when we're being courted by someone else.

If I had my way, every black child would grow up and attend a Historically Black College or University because I'd like every black high school graduate in the country to have the HBCU experience, but that dream is out of my reach. However, I know there are plenty of students already enrolled in HBCUs who are having a tough time paying for their education and I realized I could help those kids. So, instead of trying to send every black child to an HBCU, I decided to set up the Tom Joyner Foundation for the purpose of helping kids stay in HBCUs.

When we started the Tom Joyner Foundation we didn't have a building or a catchy slogan. In fact, our unofficial working slogan was "Help a kid stay in college because their parents don't want them to move back home." It's too long, but it does make the point. Hey, I put two sons through college and once they'd left home I renovated their rooms quicker than you can say "freshman dormitory."

We started the foundation with a board of people who understood and were committed to our vision; then we created a mission statement and got to work. The first step was to set up a 900 number people could call if they wanted to donate money. We asked our listeners to commit to $5 or more to help kids who are running out of money at Historically Black Colleges and Universities. The checks started rolling in immediately and the best news is, they cleared the bank! Today huge corporations donate thousands of dollars every month to the Tom Joyner Foundation. But the roots of the foundation came one check at a time. The only thing our listeners wanted in return was our assurance that the money would be put to the use it was intended for.

So far, with a big boost from our biggest fund-raiser, the

Fantastic Voyage Cruise, the Tom Joyner Foundation has raised more than $30 million, and it feels good when a student stops me and says, "Tom Joyner, I was one of the scholarship recipients" . . . especially when it happens at a college commencement ceremony. I get a lot of big hugs and, more importantly, the world gets an African American child who is probably smarter, more confident, and more excited about a future that will probably be brighter because of graduating from an HBCU. I'm just a deejay, but that's a pretty good return on an investment.

I will continue to honor my commitment to HBCUs for as long as I'm a black man, but that doesn't mean I can't look at the situation realistically and recognize the problems we face. As much as I would like Historically Black Colleges and Universities to be the beacon of hope for every black student who would like to attend one, the sad reality is that many of the schools have lost their accreditation along with federal dollars needed to provide scholarships. The students that are enrolled in the troubled schools can't afford to attend any longer and probably don't want to. The dismal state of many of the schools makes recruiting new students almost impossible.

The Tom Joyner Foundation continues to encourage kids to go to HBCUs and gives millions away to those who do, despite the sad fact that many of the institutions themselves have no future. Because of this situation, we had to find a new way to make the relationship work since the old way was like trying to fill a bucket with a hole in it. So the Tom Joyner Foundation entered the higher-education business to buy ailing schools, run them in a more efficient way, get their accreditation and federal funding back, and return them to the state of viability and importance in the community they once had. When you want something badly sometimes you really have to put yourself out there in order to get it. You ought not send someone else to represent what you want, because your stand-in might be more likely to accept no for an answer.

There's a huge misconception that students who attend HBCUs do so because they can't cut it somewhere else. Although most HBCUs do pride themselves in giving students who might have been unable to attend anywhere else a chance to get a college education, there are and always have been top-caliber students who choose HBCUs. These are usually students whose parents or mentors have shared with them the importance of choosing an HBCU. These students have a sense of what an HBCU can offer them and what they can offer an HBCU. Too often when we make decisions about our jobs, schools, churches, and lives, we're only concerned about how it will benefit us, not how we will be able to make someone else's situation more positive. We should spend more time asking ourselves what we're bringing to the table. If you're a good student or you know one, I recommend that you put an HBCU on your list of colleges. A good HBCU will take what you have and make it better.

When you find a cause, a mission, a project you're willing to see through to the end that isn't motivated by money, you'll get a feeling far better than anything any material possession can bring you. If you haven't yet found it, I challenge you to begin thinking about finding such a mission or project. I'm committed to HBCUs because I don't believe there's an educational system out there that could have done a better job at turning my two black boys into two black educated men with a sense of history and compassion for African American people. After graduating from the MBA program at Florida A&M University, my son Oscar had completed a paid internship at Procter & Gamble and had gotten job offers from more than one *Fortune* 500 company. I have no doubt that the outcome would have been similar had he graduated from any

MBA program in the country. But he wouldn't have gotten the satisfaction of getting a master's degree from the same institution his grandfather attended nor would he have felt that sense of pride any black person feels when we realize we've done something just as well as—or better than—anyone else, on our own. We need these victories, as individuals and as a race. If you want to go to a mainstream college and get an education, by all means do it. But don't do it because you believe your success will have more validity because you were educated with and by white people. Historically Black Colleges and Universities are my thing. They continue to teach me that black folks can be self-sufficient, yet competitive in mainstream America. Your thing may be something else entirely. But whatever it is, honor your commitment. No mountain or valley should keep you away.

chapter nine

"Ladies' Night"

When I was a kid, two things
were almost always on my
mind: food and girls.

I THOUGHT I was the luckiest man in the world. It was the 1980s, and hundreds of women had shown up for the "Ladies Only" engagement with the sexiest black man alive. They were dressed provocatively and they were ready to throw their panties up on the stage. Electricity filled the room and in just moments the curtain would open and the ladies would get exactly what they came for—Teddy Pendergrass.

I was just the deejay, but, hey, Teddy and I were the only males in the room, and, at least in my fantasy, one pair of those panties would come flying my way. I watched this show night after night and wondered how this experience felt to Teddy and anyone else who became a sex symbol. What was it like to have women screaming your name? I may never know, but I sure know what it's like to be standing near the target of those screams and that's good enough for me.

Over the years I had become accustomed to being practically invisible to women and the cool thing about it was if they weren't watching me, they might not notice how much I was watching them. When I was a kid, two things were almost always on my mind: food and girls. I wanted to get my hands on both of them, but food was much easier to get. So, at some point in my life, I began to try to put myself in situations, like playing music in the cafeteria and singing with the DuPonts, that would get me noticed by girls. My feelings for women developed into something that could be described as obsessive and a little quirky, I'll admit. But it didn't start out that way.

My first experiences with women were great. My mother was my pal, my confidante, and my biggest supporter. She was such a friend to me, that's why I nicknamed her Buddy. When she wasn't around, her sister, my aunt Nettie, was right there. After graduating from Tennessee State, Nettie came to live with us in Tuskegee from the time I was in kindergarten until she got married and I was in the sixth grade. After I'd get out of school I had the choice of going either to visit my mom on the agricultural side of the college that smelled like cow manure or to visit Nettie at her office in the cafeteria that smelled like biscuits, fried chicken, and okra. I spent a lot of time at Nettie's office and Buddy understood!

I had several aunts and they all were sweet and kind. From each of them I learned early on that there's no kind of hurt that a woman can't fix. Even though Buddy and Nettie have passed on, the love they gave me was so strong that it still brings me comfort to this day. When I do well, I see their smiles and when I do something they wouldn't be proud of, I can feel their disappointment. In every woman I meet, I'm reminded of those two special women, and so I always try to treat all women with a certain amount of reverence and respect.

The women in my life gave me my first lesson in unconditional love. Nettie baked an apple pie like no one else in the world. If you think you can top her, I'm willing to give your apple pie a try. My sister-in-law, Danita, thinks she has finally gotten it down and I have to admit I told her that she had. But although she is real close, it isn't Nettie's.

With my daddy, things were black or white. When I was good, I was rewarded and when I was bad, I got a beating. But whether I was good or bad, Nettie's love and apple pie were there for me. In fact, when I was in trouble, that's when I could count on Nettie most to hide me from my daddy. When she married and moved out, I would go to her house when I'd stayed out past my curfew. Not only would she cover for me, she'd stand boldly before my daddy and tell him I had been at her house the whole time, even though my clothes were loaded with dirt and grass stains and I smelled like a wet puppy!

Because my mama and my aunts were so good to me, I was shocked to discover one day that all females weren't as kind. As special as I was to Nettie and Buddy, I was equally "unspecial" to the girls in my town. To be more specific, I was nasty. How nasty was I? My nickname was Fungus. I think I was labeled as a "nasty boy" because my search to see girl's underwear was almost as intense as my search for an apple pie as good as Nettie's. Now before you judge me too harshly, consider my predicament. I was a young, fat boy in a small town back in the day before regular magazines had underwear ads. There were no video girls, no Internet, barely any suggestive music on the radio. You might think living in a home with such beautiful, wholesome, respectable women would lead me to desire those qualities in the girls I'd come across, but that wasn't the case at all. I had soft and sweet at home—now, I was looking for fast!

Being a mama's boy works well for me now. It has a whole different connotation today than it had when I was a kid. Back in the day, it kept me from getting any play. You had to be rough and tough to get the girls' attention. I recently met a young woman who told me her mom had gone to college with me. When I figured out who her mom was and how fine she was, I didn't even have to ask. I *knew* she'd had nothing to do with me.

As I've gotten older and more successful, I've been smart enough to realize that the same women who wouldn't give me the time of day when I was plain old nasty Tom have become much more likely to say hello to me now—and that's just fine with me. I don't hold it against them. I'm just grateful that they've finally come around! When I go home to Tuskegee, some of the same girls who snubbed me say, "Hey, Tom, remember me?" and give a big hug. Whether I remember them or not, I take those hugs gladly.

I hear guys say they had it rough because they were always relegated to the role of being just a "friend" to the girls they grew up with; I would have gladly accepted that position. What I was to most girls was absolutely nothing. Now that I have, after many years, accumulated a lot of female friends and employees, even though it's probably not the politically correct thing to do, I can't treat women like one of the guys. Women aren't guys, thank goodness, and there's no way I can allow one I'm with to carry something that's too heavy or open a door. Again, it's partly because they're soft and sweet like Buddy and Nettie and partly because they're wearing underwear.

You can never give a woman too many compliments or show her too much kindness. I may not always know what women want but it isn't because I'm not trying to figure it out. Valentine's Day is my favorite holiday and every woman in my life knows that beginning with the first day of February, it's on! I cannot be responsible for what I might do or say because I am literally blinded by love. Not only is it the month of Buddy's birth, it's also Black History Month, it's when Donna and I first met face-to-face, and it's our wedding anniversary. Now, if you save your old *Ebony* magazines, you might think we got married in July. We did. But first, back in February, we snuck off and held a private ceremony on Valentine's Day. Then later, in July, we had a huge wedding and party in Jamaica. It was so nice, we did it twice. So, if I promise anything in the month of February, everyone close to me knows to check its validity in March.

One Valentine's tradition that I instituted, and actually has been expanded to other parts of the year as well, is our visits to women's shelters. After all, who needs love more than women and their families who have been victims of domestic abuse? For years we've tried to brighten a few of their days with candy, personal items, toys for the kids, and—what puts a smile on every woman's face—knockoff Louis Vuitton purses and luggage. The reaction we get when we spend a few hours making these women feel as special as they deserve to feel is one of pure gratitude. If you have a chance to make someone's day, take it. A few moments out of your life could change someone else's forever.

My daddy gets most of the credit for teaching me the importance of working hard and accomplishing goals. But it was Buddy who taught me to be compassionate, have concern for others, and to try to find some good in everyone I meet. I learned it from the way she lived her life. She was always opening our home to students who needed help writing papers, and doing what she could to make certain they had what was needed to meet the challenges they faced. It was her influence that led us to start the Tom Joyner Foundation, which raises money for kids at Historically Black Colleges and Universities.

Most mothers are special to their sons, and my former wife, Dora, is no exception. Dora instilled in our boys the importance of remembering where they came from. As our income increased over the years and we were able to afford the finer things in life, like a nice home and private schools, she never allowed these things to change who our sons were. She taught them to be thankful and grateful for what they had and kept them grounded through their involvement in the church they'd grown up in.

No matter how far away you get from home, and no matter whom you meet, there's nothing like singing in the youth choir in dark slacks and a white shirt to help remind you that things haven't changed that much. When people tell me what nice, well-rounded, down-to-earth guys my sons have turned out to be, I will always give Dora her due. While I was out of the home working to provide a certain type of lifestyle, she was at home in the trenches providing love, morality, stability, and rides to soccer, Little League, and football practices. If there's a Supermom cape out there, it goes to her. I was persistent about following my dreams and desires to become a success, and if Dora hadn't held things down on the home front, the outcome would have been much different.

Even though it happens that my only sibling, my children, my business partners, and my cook are all males, the core group of people I depend on from day to day are women. On the *Morning Show*, Sybil, Myra J., Jedda Jones (Ms. Dupre), Mary Boyce, Julia Atherton, Katrina Witherspoon, Stephnie Williams, Michelle Webb, Tanita Buni, Kim Nelson-Ingram, Erica Taylor, Janyce Brannon, Barbara Harrington, and Andrell Perry are all crucial to me and to the show. They're smart, strong, dependable, and fun and they know they can get just about anything out of me in the month of February.

Over at Reach Media there are just too many women to single out, but suffice it to say there are more women than men. I can't take full credit for that because most of the staff was hired by my son Oscar, but I'm pleased with his choices. I like to work with people who are happy to be working, and honestly I think it's more difficult for men to let other men know they want to work for them. There always seems to be some level of competition going on and men are much more likely to try to prove how much they can accomplish without me. Admitting dependency, especially on another male, for some guys is a sign of weakness. I don't spend a lot of time worrying about it and in the end my relationship with women has worked to my advantage personally and professionally. My having spent all that time thinking about women when I couldn't get any has, on the personal side, helped me to understand them a lot better than some fellow members of the male species. What was once considered to be obsessive and borderline weird is now counted as being sensitive and attentive. And some of what was nasty is now romantic . . . well, some, not all. And professionally, since the bulk of my audience is female, giving them what they want will always be a recipe for success. Women control the radio and the television whether their men choose to believe it or not, so it's my job, first and foremost, to serve them.

If you're a man with women in your life, whether you have a radio show or not, I suggest that you do the same. Treat women with love, respect, and dignity every day. Make them feel special, because they are.

chapter ten

"Papa's Got a Brand New Bag"

If you're a father or a son, or
both, give yourself and your
dad a break. Love one another
with all the love
you know how to give, and
make every moment
together count.

BEING THE children of "the Hardest Working Man in Radio" was no picnic for my two sons, Killer and Thriller. The fact that I was a popular radio deejay meant no more to them than if I had been a popular mail sorter at the post office. In fact, sometimes I think that would have suited them better. Then at least they wouldn't have had to get teased by their classmates when I discussed on the air the funny things they'd done or said.

When they got old enough to let me know they were serious about their discomfort, they asked me not to talk about them on the radio anymore and I obliged them. Meanwhile, off the air I thought a lot about all the time I was spending away from them. Their childhood in Dallas was a lot different from mine in Tuskegee, even though many of the dynamics were very similar. Like my brother and me, they were two male siblings growing up together in a two-parent household. But even though I tried to have a strong presence when I was home—attending their games and parent-teacher meetings, etc.—and had no problem tearing up their behinds when the situation arose, in my mind, I wasn't the traditional father and I wondered how that would affect my boys.

My grueling schedule as a morning deejay in Dallas and an afternoon deejay in Chicago kept me away from home for the entire day and most nights five days a week. As Killer and Thriller grew to be young men I wasn't sure what they learned from me other than how not to miss a plane. I give their mother, Dora, most of the credit for the bright, conscientious men they became. But after they graduated from college and returned to Dallas and the three of us began to work together on a day-to-day basis, I began to realize something. The old cliché that it's the quality of time and not the quantity of time that counts proved to have been true. Thomas and Oscar both are hard workers and are dedicated to helping and improving the lives of black people, and even though I don't remember saying that's what they should do, I'd like to believe they saw me live my life that way. They also know, without a doubt, that I loved them and was there for them. The mutual love and respect the three of us have for one another is something I'll cherish forever. Of course, there are also some things about them I don't understand at all and cannot take credit or blame for.

Thomas is a huge trivia buff. That's a nice way of saying his head is full of useless information that not too many people really care about. Thank goodness he married Toy, a woman who doesn't seem to mind when he points out the hotel in Baltimore where a drug deal on the TV show *The Wire* actually went down. One of his dreams is to become a contestant on *Jeopardy!* If they have a category on Sly Stone, he'll clean up! As a young kid, Thomas became fascinated with the former lead singer of Sly and the Family Stone and knows way too much about the man. Thankfully, I had more influence on the man Thomas would become than Sly did!

Oscar is very headstrong and committed to any endeavor he undertakes—no matter how bleak the situation may look to the people around him. Whether it was the Saab he was pouring money into or the singing group he managed, giving up was not in his vocabulary. It ain't over until Oscar says it's over. Another thing about him is he knows everything about business. I'm not saying he knows a lot about business or he's very knowledgeable about business. I'm saying he knows EVERYTHING about business. I've never seen a person so young so confident about something so new to him. To say that his MBA from Florida A&M got him prepared to run a business is a major understatement. His MBA from Florida A&M got him prepared to run the world—oh yeah, and me too. I work for him now. So I'm glader than ever that he was raised to be fair, honest, and willing to work hard for what he plans to achieve in life.

When parents ask me for advice about raising their kids, I say, raise them with the idea that you may be working for them one day. The day my sons and I started working together was one of my happiest moments, but it was a day I never saw coming.

While Thomas and Oscar were away in college and I was busy getting the syndicated radio show off the ground in the early '90s, I got to know Eddie Levert of the group the O'Jays. Eddie had the life I wished I had. I would see him with his sons, Gerald, Sean, and Eddie Jr., and I thought he was the luckiest guy in the world. Here was a guy who had been hugely successful in his musical career, and his sons had followed him into the business. Eddie Jr. helped him on the road and Gerald and Sean had successful singing careers. How cool was that, I thought, to have a job that you love and to have your sons right by your side, working with you and hanging out with you almost on a daily basis?

I knew that when those boys of his were young, Eddie was on the road most of the time; in fact, he was away from them more than I was away from my sons. How did he pull this off? I found myself feeling tinges of jealousy over the fact that his boys dug him and respected his career so much. My boys hadn't grown up hanging around the radio stations I'd worked at, and even if they had, radio wasn't really the kind of business you wanted your kids to follow you into. There's hardly any job security, and to be honest, I knew they had higher aspirations. Plus, it's not likely that the three of us could have done a radio show together even if they had shown the slightest interest. Thomas had been thinking of becoming a lawyer and Oscar had announced in the tenth grade that he was going to run a marketing company, Joyner and Associates, even though, at the time, neither he nor I had any idea what Joyner and Associates would possibly market or produce.

Fast-forward to the year 1998 when I decided to form the Tom Joyner Foundation to raise money for kids who had run out of money at HBCUs. We were giving away thousands of dollars a week to outstanding moms and dads and we were getting a lot of calls from students who were having a tough time paying for college. Historically Black Colleges and Universities were something near and dear to my heart and I knew I wanted to find a way to become involved with them. I remembered how my mom would help students from Tuskegee get their term papers, theses, and dissertations ready and how she never turned any student in need away. My brother Albert, my dad, my mom, both sets of grandparents, and my sons were all graduates of HBCUs. Albert, my dad, and my sons all agreed that nothing would have made Buddy prouder than for me to create a way to give back to students at black colleges.

Thomas, who may possibly love HBCUs just as much as I do, was the perfect person to run the foundation, and lo and behold, I had a son working with me. At this point, the radio show was doing well and it was becoming clear that we were ready to branch out into other areas of communications, like the Internet. We decided an Internet news service with news and information from the black perspective was the direction we'd take. BlackAmericaWeb.com was launched, and thankfully we didn't go with the name proposed by Thomas, Drop That Chicken! I'll admit it got across the message of urgency that our news stories would have, and it was catchy—but it wasn't very dignified.

Oscar would soon get his business degree. There was no doubt in my mind that he was competent to run Black AmericaWeb.com and the other entities that would fall under the company. Reach Media Inc. was born a couple years later and was designed to encompass BlackAmericaWeb.com, and everything else that falls under the Tom Joyner brand name. Finally, the three of us, Thomas, Oscar, and I were a team, and even though we're not a singing group, our harmony is on par with Eddie Levert and his boys.

I'd like to believe my relationship with my boys is better than the one I had with my daddy. My brother, Albert, was the better student and the athlete of the family and, I believe, the kind of son Pops really wanted. Since I was a "mama's boy" I was busy hanging out with Buddy and making sure my daddy was treating her "right." And I know that kept us from being as close as we probably could have been when I was growing up. Of course he denies it, but there are some things I remember him doing when I was a kid that the man he appears to be now would never do.

For example, on a family vacation to New York City, as our family was going to board the subway, my mama and I got stuck. Not because I was too fat, but because my daddy made the two of us go through the same turnstile. When the authorities stopped Buddy and me, that mean, cheap man and my brother, Albert, kept walking as though they didn't know us. I was terrified, believing Buddy and I would be thrown in jail in of all places, New York City! When I brought it up to him not long ago, Pops said he doesn't remember that ever happening. In his mid-eighties he chose to recall only the good times and I guess I can't fault him for that. There were a lot more good times than bad, and when a black man can say that after eighty plus years, he deserves a pat on the back—and the right to try to change if he can.

I'm telling you, the man my father became late in life is *not* the man who raised me. He's transformed himself into a kind old grandpa and I'm glad I met him. When I was a kid I could depend on him to provide for us and to discipline us, but I always had the feeling he had a tough time expressing his feelings. Later he became a huge supporter of both our careers. In fact, he is my unofficial archivist. He keeps every newspaper and magazine article that I've been featured in and even has my television appearances on videotape. I dial him up from the car every morning around 4:30 a.m. on the way to the radio station and sometimes out of the blue he'll say, "Son, I was just watching you on the *60 Minutes* interview again . . . it was pretty good." It's a reminder to me that he really is proud of me and it's also reminder that when you get old you can't sleep. Well, I guess if you've got to be up all night going to the bathroom, if you're having good thoughts about your kids, it's a pretty good trade-off.

It's a blessing for me to be able to share the fruits of my success with my sons and my daddy. When the four of us traveled to South Africa in the 1990s it was just one of the many opportunities the three generations of Joyner men had to bond and it was a high point in all of our lives. Of course, we spend less time bonding when we're together and more time making sure the family's patriarch isn't making inappropriate moves on fine young women he happens to meet along the way. In fact, if you're a woman under fifty and fine, let me apologize right now for anything my daddy might have done or said if you've met him! He is truly living his life to the fullest, and as embarrassing as it is sometimes, I have to give him his props.

When it became clear that Pops needed a little more assistance but couldn't really be tied down at an independent living facility, we bought him a home in Dallas where he could have his privacy and keep his dignity, and get the medical attention he would inevitably need. The house, right up the street from Donna and me, was formerly owned by TV psychologist Dr. Phil. While his relocating from Alabama, the state where he'd lived for sixty years, was an emotional transition, it began a new and positive chapter in the lives of the Joyner men. At first, my biggest fear was to pass his house on my way to work before dawn and catch him walking a young, fine "lady friend" to her car!

There's no blueprint for fatherhood, or for that matter "sonhood." You can compare yourselves to others and wish things could be different, but I've learned that if you just do your best, everything works out in the end. The example you set will make a difference in your life and in generations to come and in ways you may not expect. If you're a father or a son, or both, give yourself and your dad a break. Love one another with all the love you know how to give, and make every moment together count.

When my daddy needed a computer a few years ago, he didn't come to me. He went to Thomas Jr. and the two of them figured out what he needed. That's their relationship. A lot of people like to collect heirlooms and family hand-me-downs. That isn't me at all. I'm more interested in contemporary stuff. But when my son Oscar bought his first home he asked Pops if he could have the old pool table he had in his home in Tuskegee for years. I don't know how much my daddy paid for that pool table but it couldn't have cost as much as it cost to ship it from Alabama to Texas, yet Oscar was determined to make it happen and he did. If you ask him why he'll tell you: because it was Granddad's.

chapter eleven

"What's Love Got to Do with It?"

It has recently been "discovered" that fat people get less sleep than thin people. Duh! We're up eating.

ALL OF a sudden the whole world is concerned about weight. You can't turn on the TV or the radio without some type of weight-loss program being advertised. Atkins, South Beach, Weight Watchers, Jenny Craig, Slim-Fast, it's all out there for people who have discovered they're overweight. Ha! Finally everyone else is dealing with what I've been dealing with all my life . . . fat. I was the fat kid. It wasn't a stigma, it wasn't a curse, it wasn't even a problem. It was just the way it was. People who didn't know me back then ask, "Were you really fat or were you plump?" You can call it whatever you want to, chubby, husky, chunky, it all means the same thing . . . fat.

As a former fat kid and a current fat man I'm noticing that our society is making it much too easy to be overweight. Don't get me started on the money that's being spent on studying us and coming up with psychological reasons for why we're the way we are. Have you heard of the patch that makes people feel full? Good luck. Fat people don't eat food because we're hungry. We eat food because it's there. It has recently been "discovered" that fat people get less sleep than thin people. Duh! We're up eating. As long as Domino's delivers late into the night, we'll be up! Hey, convenience stores and doughnut shops that are open all night can't be helping our waistlines.

Even cars are getting bigger and wider. If we were forced to ride around in cars the size of Ford Pintos we'd be thinner, plus because they broke down so much, we'd have less money to spend on snacks.

There are also studies that tell us things that are painfully obvious—like there are more fat people now than ever. I know. But being a fat kid in today's world is different from being fat back in the day. It's much more acceptable now, and instead of kids' getting yelled at for it, their parents and teachers try to understand what the causes are. Lack of exercise, stress, slow metabolism, nervous eating, poor nutrition, are all excuses that are acceptable today. Fat kids receive positive feedback from experts for their condition and appear on daytime talk shows. The only feedback I got was "Put that down!" "Didn't you have seconds?" "Close that refrigerator!"

Thanks mostly to kids sitting on their behinds playing video games instead of tag, there are a lot of fat kids in school today. When I was a fat kid there was just one or two of us. I guess looking back at it, we were "special," but no one made us feel like it. Thank goodness, I never really let it get me down. Hey, no one had any sympathy for me, and in retrospect that was good. That meant I had to do everything the thin kids did even if I couldn't always do it as well. I played football, basketball, swam, and even participated in every fat kid's nightmare—dodgeball! So, I was fat but I was healthy because I got plenty of exercise.

Because there weren't as many fat people back then, we didn't know fat was causing so much trouble. Today we know it's killing us in all sorts of ways. Most of the illnesses that plague the African American community, hypertension (the pressure), diabetes (the sugar), and heart disease, are directly related to obesity. If we could get our weight under control, we might find that all kinds of sicknesses and conditions that so many of us suffer with would almost disappear, or would become at least more manageable and less life-threatening.

I was the only fat person in my family, so I had to work hard at maintaining my level of fatness. I really loved food and I thought about it a lot. Visions of cookies and cake constantly danced in my head. Actually they still do. But kids today have an abundance of bad food around them. If you're a parent, the least you can do is make your kids work for their snacks. Parents are their kids' enablers these days. Not only do you bring unhealthy food into the home, you drive your family right to it, sometimes several times a week. The next time you're in a drive-thru line at a fast-food restaurant, think of what a steady diet of fried food is doing to your children. And then consider going inside the restaurant so at least they can get the benefit of walking off a couple of calories.

IF WE don't get this obesity issue under control we're going to be in a world of trouble, and not just with our health. We have enough problems getting a fair shake in this society and obesity just adds on another layer. Employers will find ways to get around hiring overweight people because it ends up costing them more. Since overweight people have more health issues, insurance costs are higher and theoretically they miss more days of work. I hate to always play the race card, but I play the hand I'm dealt. White people are figuring this weight thing out and if we're not careful the technology gap and the health gap are going to be joined by the fat gap . . . another area where we're being left behind as a group. Our communities are the ones filled with restaurants selling fried chicken, fried burgers, and fried fish with few healthy alternatives. The hood is where you have to go to find fatback, pigs' feet, chittlins, etc. It's not to say that white people don't indulge in unhealthy lifestyles, but it isn't in their faces as much.

Getting black people to become more proactive about their health was the goal of "Take a Loved One to the Doctor Day," an event we began as a partnership with the former secretary of health Tommy Thompson. As the name implies, it's a day set aside once a year where we encourage our listeners to take someone they love to the doctor. Of all the promotions we've done in the past meant to help black people, this one was truly a lifesaver. Health fairs were set up in most of the cities where the *Tom Joyner Morning Show* is heard and our entire staff participated in Doctor Day along with the millions of listeners and their families.

My son Oscar learned he had diabetes at our first Doctor Day and other members of our crew discovered ailments they didn't know they had. J. Anthony Brown, who had publicly dealt with his diabetes for years, was a constant reminder that the disease could be managed if you ate right, lost weight, and took your medicine. Sharing his ongoing battle with the disease has helped many of our listeners along the way.

Moving, personal testimonies from Doctor Day participants have made it a success in every sense of the word. Too many of us are afraid to go to the doctor or don't have the money or insurance to get the treatment we need. That means by the time we do see a medical professional, often the disease has moved from something that could have been managed to something that is going to kill us. That reality hits close to home. Many years before women were urged to get yearly mammograms, breast cancer took my aunt Nettie quickly. Sybil Wilkes's mom and aunts, and J. Anthony Brown's mom and dad all died of cancer. "Take a Loved One to the Doctor Day" I think is our way of paying tribute to those loved ones we wish we could have helped save.

Oh, and here's a praise report. Oscar changed his diet and a year later on a visit to the doctor he learned he had no more signs of the disease.

None of us are invincible. Over the past few years the same

diseases that affect our friends and relatives have been slowing
down or killing some of our most beloved entertainers. "The
Late" is a label I hate putting in front anyone's name, and
adding it to Barry White's was especially hard. Barry White
and stroke victims Luther Vandross and Ron Isley are re-
minders that diseases like diabetes don't care who you are and
they're nothing to play around with. You've got to improve
your diet, take your medication, exercise, and lose weight before it's too late. Especially if these illnesses run in your family.
Ron Isley had lost family members already from diabetes and
Luther had practically lost his entire immediate family—his
father, his sister, and a brother.

I hate dieting and exercise and I don't get a kick out of
drinking several bottles of water every day. Boxing is something I do enjoy but it is rigorous and there are plenty of days
I don't feel like doing it. I exercise because I want to be as
healthy as I can be so that I can do the things I want to do in
life—and still feel twenty-three years old. The best thing I can
personally say about exercise is that it is what brought Donna
and me together. Before I met Donna Richardson I'd seen her
on TV doing her workouts and in fitness magazines. I'd never
actually worked out while watching her on ESPN, but I did
sit on the couch and eat oatmeal cookies, which is the second
best thing you can do when you're alone sitting on the couch
watching a fine woman do lunges. Eventually, she became my
trainer, my friend, my traveling companion, and my wife. I've
always ended up hating my trainers, so before it came to that,
we decided to sever our trainer-trainee relationship and stick
to being plain old husband and wife. That's not to say she still
doesn't try to police my eating. She keeps a stash of cookies
somewhere in the house and doles them out to me like I'm a
puppy getting treats. As undignified as it is, I never turn them
down.

Of all the challenges I've faced in my life, my battle with weight is one that has been the toughest, and I know this is something I have in common with a large number of our audience. I can make fat jokes about Gerald Levert, the Pine Sol Lady, and Fred Hammond because we're all in the same club. Years ago, while the *Tom Joyner* crew was on the road I overheard someone say, "Now that's a Big show." She wasn't talking about the A-list of people performing, the size of the set, or the investment we'd put into production—she was talking about us. We're all struggling with it, we're all looking for answers, we're all wondering if black really makes us look slimmer.

In reality, I think we spend way too much time worrying about our outward appearances and make some bad and sometimes hurtful decisions based on people's weight. The important thing is what's going on in the inside, and that goes back to feeling good. Instead of trying to get skinny, let's shoot for healthy, and if a healthy lifestyle causes you to shed some pounds, cool.

Our bodies really are our temples and we only get one. If we take steps toward making better choices about our food and exercise we'll live longer and happier lives. We have enough information linking certain foods and certain behaviors to poor health and we're intelligent enough to begin making the choices that will keep us from suffering and dying unnecessarily.

Food plays a big role in almost everything we take part in as a family—holidays, birthdays, graduation parties, baby showers, and funerals. We've even added new traditions that are centered on food like Super Bowl parties and "June Bug Is Out of Jail Again" celebrations—any excuse for a big spread will do. Even things that really have nothing to do with food, like book club meetings, have become places where buffalo wings and cake are practically mandatory.

We love food but we're consuming too much of it, and too much of the wrong things. If you have a gathering that includes huge, heavy meals, do like Donna's family does afterward. Her mom, Miss LaVerne, and her aunts put on some music, move the furniture back, and dance. If you're going to try this, be sure to include physical old-school dances like the Pony, the Shake, the Jerk, the Swim, the Skate . . . go up the '80s with the Cabbage Patch and the Running Man, and then cool down with the "over forty dance," just popping your fingers and moving lightly from side to side. Whatever you do, don't make your whole family dance only new school. Standing in place bobbing your head up and down and moving one arm up and down looks cool, but does nothing for your cardiovascular system.

Family reunions are another excellent opportunity to include dancing, games, and activities that get the heart pumping. Start your own family line dance like "the Jones Family Slide." Every year add a new step and make it simple enough so the white date some family member will inevitably bring to the reunion can catch on too.

Come up with some fun games the whole family can join in and play. Have relay races and instead of passing batons pass rib bones. Here's a warning about the family games—use some discretion. If Aunt Ruby is seventy-seven you might not want to make her the anchor in a game of tug-of-war, but then again, I don't know your aunt Ruby!

Even if you're at home and you're enjoying a big meal with your spouse, when you've finished eating, your wife can hide the TV remote in her blouse while you chase her around the house—hey, it works for us!

Giving up everything you enjoy eating, however, will never

work and will just keep you frustrated trying all kinds of diets and fads, so don't waste your time making unrealistic goals about nutrition and exercise. We need to pull up a bit and add more balance. Don't give up on fried foods altogether, just cut back. If your plate has fried chicken, french fries, fried green tomatoes, and fried cheesecake (I swear that's a real recipe), you're in too deep! If Big Mama thinks the world will end if she doesn't start the new year with chittlins, hog head cheese, and a huge pot of black-eyed peas with a big pig foot inside, let her do her thing. One day out of the year of that kind of eating won't kill anyone. We just can't continue to eat like that all year long. If you know you're not well, you need to have sense enough to refuse certain things. I never want to hear anyone say, "Bring me my medication and a pig ear sandwich." The two just don't go together.

If you haven't yet begun eating bad, don't start. If you're a young person or the parent of young children, the best thing you can do is begin a healthy regimen now. I know it's hard to think that way when you're young and fine, but take a look around you. If you have older family members who are taking blood pressure medication, on dialysis, struggling with their weight, etc., you have to believe that's going to be your legacy unless you take control of your health right now.

If you're young and thin and don't believe you're going to gain weight, look at some old family photos or high school yearbooks and compare the pictures to the way those people look now—and don't laugh at the Jheri curls. In twenty years your phony ponytail is going to be pretty funny to your children.

Everything you do to your body catches up to you. Bad food, drugs, alcohol, cigarettes—all will have an impact down the road. It's not only about obesity. There are a lot of skinny people with health problems too. If you're already at risk for some of the conditions that I've been talking about or already have been diagnosed, get help and follow your physician's orders. Let's all make good health a priority. Take a loved one to the doctor, especially if that loved one is you.

chapter twelve

"MoneyMoneyMoneyMoneyMoney"

*There are a lot of strange
and unfair things about
money I've discovered over the
years, like the more you have,
the more free stuff you get.*

A FEW years ago, I was in Chicago working on a project in January. It was freezing cold. I'm a warm-weather kind of guy and spend as little time as possible in places where the temperature drops below zero. My business dealings wrapped up early unexpectedly and I wanted to get back to Dallas. I was sitting there thinking about buying an American Airlines ticket back home and how I'd probably have to at least stay overnight to keep from having to pay a huge price for that ticket. I sat there for about an hour before it dawned on me, "Hey! I'm rich! I can get a ticket right now and be home in time to catch Judge Mablean."

I love money. I know you're not supposed to admit it, I know the love of money is the root of all evil, and I know it can't buy happiness or love, but I love it anyway. And here's why: I've finally figured out how to use it. Oh, I know—I can hear you now. "Give it to me, Tom Joyner! I know what to do with it!"

We all think that, but trust me, it isn't true. I've heard preachers say to congregations, "You haven't learned to take care of the little money you have now—why would God bless you with a lot more?" Good point. Of course, some of those same preachers have been asking for money for the same building fund for the past thirty years. I guess maybe God is waiting for them to learn to take care of what they have before he blesses them with more. Can I get an Amen?

How many people do you know who have gotten their hands on a huge sum of money and blown it? The answer is probably every one of them. It's almost a rite of passage. You *will* blow your first fortune. For some it's the last chance they get; for others they work faster and harder and are a lot more careful so they can prove they can handle the big bucks. Thankfully, I was in the latter category.

There are two kinds of fortunes—the kind you win and the kind you earn. You'll still blow a lot of it the first time either way, but at least if you earn it you have a better chance of doing what you did the first time to make it back.

Back in the 1970s I worked for Muhammad Ali. My relationship began with the Champ while I was a deejay at radio station KKDA in Dallas. I sent a telegram to him after his belt had been taken by the boxing commission because he refused to serve in the Vietnam War. I started calling him on the phone and he would speak on the air. He was impressed at how I was always able to track him down in places like Manila and Zaire. He liked me and he liked doing the telephone segments on my morning show. Even though he hadn't met me yet, three or four times he gave me a shout-out after a match.

Now you have to understand, Ali gave almost everyone a shout-out. He'd first thank Allah, then his manager Herbert Muhammad. After that it was a free-for-all. He'd shout out to a person he'd met at a truck stop, and a woman he'd met at the grocery store. But the few times he thanked Tom Joyner in Dallas, Texas, I have to admit I felt twenty feet tall.

In January 1975, Ali came to Dallas and paid a visit to the radio station. We hit it off and the next thing I knew, a man who wanted to start a syndicated sports radio talk show hosted by the Champ offered me a job as a producer. The catch was, the Champ knew nothing about it. The deal was: If I could convince the Champ to sign the contract, I would get a $50,000 signing bonus and about $200,000 to come later. The man might as well have said $200 million . . . *all* that money was already spent in my head. My response was "Shoot yeah!"

I talked to Ali, he liked the deal, and we signed the contract in Chicago. I returned to Dallas and when I got my "fortune" I quit my radio job at KKDA and had another huge parade.

I joined Ali at his farm and spent two weeks with him trying every day to get him to read scripts into my tape recorder. He put me off every morning until he finally confessed that he didn't want to do the sports show. I was devastated. Devastated because I was going to be out of work and because Ali suggested that we return the money we'd gotten for signing the deal. But I had already spent the $50 grand.

As soon as I got the money I jogged to the Lincoln Mercury dealership and bought a $30,000 Lincoln Mark IV. Next I went out to the cheap furniture store and paid a lot of money for some cheap-"A" furniture and moved my young family into a three-story apartment. Now, just three weeks later, the deal had fallen apart. If you ever get a lump sum of money and aren't sure that you'll be getting more, don't take out a lot of loans—pay cash.

And let me take a second to talk to you about notes and loans. If the interest rate on something you're financing is higher than the legal drinking age, walk away. I know it's tempting to pay $40 a month for a big-screen TV, but do the math and read the fine print. Rent-to-own, cash-and-carry, tote-the-note—almost anything hyphenated is going to be a high-interest trap for people who don't have a lot of money to spend. But if you don't have a lot of money to spend sometimes you think it's your only option. It isn't your only option but you'll figure that out only after you end up paying $14,000 for a $500 five-piece black lacquer bedroom set.

Here's my rule about money: I only worry about my own.

And I think you should too. But most people get upset when others "mismanage" their own money. Hey, you learn from your mistakes. Money is made to be earned and spent. Capitalism is a beautiful thing. Spending it encourages you to want to make it. Rappers who drive around in tricked-out Escalades are actually living proof of what earning a living can get you. A lot of people think they're sending the wrong messages to kids, but that isn't necessarily so. Seeing someone they relate to living large gets making money on the minds of young people and that's a good thing. Most kids can associate money only with material things. That's why, even though there may be some better financially successful role models out there, someone like a fifty-two-year-old pediatrician with a hefty portfolio and a Volvo just isn't as exciting as a twenty-two-year-old rolling on gold-plated spinners and singing about owning a $1,000 bottle of Cognac. It's our job as parents to find out how important material things are to our children and whether their desire to have money is off balance with their ability to earn it. Naturally, not every young person who aspires to own a $100,000 SUV will have the talent to produce a hit rap song, but he may figure out how to earn the money another way.

I'm a witness that there are many ways to make a lot of money legally, but we don't seem to want to give young people that much credit. If you recognize that your kids are interested in high-ticket items, why not take that opportunity to start teaching them about money? Why not find out what their interests are and start making plans for their future careers? The sooner you put the idea into their young heads that hard work and money go hand in hand, the better. And if you're leading by example, even better! But when we're living way above our means we're teaching our kids to expect immediate gratification without worrying about the consequences. All we're doing is passing down our bad spending habits.

Statistics show that African Americans don't save as much as we ought to. It's difficult to save money when you're busy trying make ends meet, but some of us who are in a position to put some money away don't do it mainly because we're not in the habit of it. The experts say to take 10 or 20 percent off the top of your paycheck and put it aside for yourself. If you also tithe at your church you have to decide whether you have 10 percent more to deduct from your salary. Talk to God about it. I'm just telling you what I've heard.

There are a lot of strange and unfair things about money I've discovered over the years, like the more you have, the more free stuff you get. People begin to offer you free stuff and then you begin to expect free stuff and everything is cool. But when you're poor and get free stuff it's frowned upon and you're accused of becoming too dependent on others.

Money can also be deceiving. It can't buy friendship, but it can cause people to be very friendly toward you. It can't buy beauty, but it can pay for a lot of plastic surgery and designer clothes, and people say you look good whether you do or not. It can't buy health but it can allow you to live a healthier lifestyle. My lifelong struggle with weight has been made easier because everywhere I go I'm accompanied by my chef and my trainer. It's something I learned from Oprah, who also literally pays the price to keep the weight off. I say this not to discourage you if you can't afford these luxuries but to let you know that, if I keep doing well financially, I might look like LL Cool J in about three years! There are only two kinds of people who have four hours a day to devote to getting fit— rich people and people in prison. Which brings me to my next topic: rich people and prison.

Because wealthy people can afford better legal representation than poor people, it's often true that we're able to use our money to get out of some sticky situations. O.J. and Kobe were able to get the best defense teams money could buy and they stayed out of jail. But having a lot of money had the opposite effect on Martha Stewart. Not only did the *court* convict her for insider trading and lying to a grand jury, but so did most of the country. The cold part is people were glad to see her go to jail mainly because she was rich. It tickled the heck out of people that this wealthy woman who had the best of everything would be spending time behind bars.

Many people I talked to about it said, in essence, "This chick goes around thinking she's perfect and above the law just because she has money and now she sees that she has to answer to the legal system just like anybody else." Then they punctuated it with the black version of "You reap what you sow," which is "That's what she gets!"

The problem is no one really knows whether she was going around thinking she was perfect, or thinking she didn't have to answer to the legal system; but these are things people tend to assume about you when you have money. Your misfortune is usually amusing. If your Pontiac Sunbird breaks down on the side of the road, you may get sympathy from people passing by, but if your Jaguar stalls, it cracks people up. That's just human nature, and rich people who get upset about it have forgotten that before they acquired money, they would have been laughing at a driver with a broken-down Jag too!

Bill Cosby, one of the wealthiest, most generous, most beloved black entertainers and philanthropists around, made a lot of black people angry when he publicly said poor people need to try to do better. I don't think they were angry because Bill Cosby criticized poor people, I think they were angry because Bill Cosby was rich and criticized poor people.

"He has his nerve!" they said. "What does he know about

being poor?" The answer is he knows a whole lot about it. He grew up very poor—in fact, he describes it as "embarrassingly poor." So poor that as a young teen he would go out with a group of his friends and when they'd stop to eat he would pretend to be full because he didn't have enough money for a burger. He's demonstrated over the years how to earn, manage, and maintain millions while still being a compassionate, stand-up black man. But to some black people, he blew it.

Money is said to be power and it is. Having it allows you to go places and see and do things you'd never otherwise get to do and see, and that's a good thing, sort of. Some rich people abuse their power. They get angry quickly and talk down to people in the service industry. If you're at a nice hotel or department store and the line is too long, some wealthy people get very upset with the clerks and complain loudly. I hate to see people who have money do something that might cause the firing of someone who doesn't have a lot of money. If a cashier, a waitress, a bellman—anyone in the service area—gets in a jam and can't "serve" to the fullest capacity, I say let it go. I don't take down names, ask to see supervisors, or give dirty looks. And for those of you who are saying, "Aren't you encouraging a poor work ethic?" No. I'm encouraging employment. All of us have a bad day now and then, and I don't want to be the person responsible for putting someone out of work, especially if that person has anything to do with the food I'm going to be eating.

Money and power also seem to make some people take part in some bizarre behavior—the richer they get, the freakier they get.

I once brought some of the *Tom Joyner Morning Show* crew to Jamaica, where we decided to charter a boat and visit an exclusive hotel called Hedonism. In retrospect, the name alone should have tipped us off. We were having dinner when an elderly white couple came over to our table and struck up a conversation. Myra J. and Ms. Dupre spent a few moments talking to them until the couple retired to their room. "They were so sweet," Myra and Ms. Dupre told me. "They've been married for over fifty years. They gave us their phone number and invited us all up to their room." The bell seemed to go off in both of their heads at the same time and the look on my face confirmed it. Let's just say the octogenarians weren't asking us up for bingo. They were swingers and decided to approach us for an evening of God knows what! Another thing money does is give you a lot of nerve!

Some rich people run out of normal things to do with their money and start spending it on crazy things. I will never understand this phenomenon, but I think the best way to keep your spending from getting too weird is to keep some people around you who knew you before you had money. They will usually keep you from doing dumb things. I often wonder where Tito was when Michael Jackson bought the bones of the Elephant Man. If I had tried something like that, my brother, Albert, would have cussed me out!

Since money can make you feel powerful, if you're a black person, it can sometimes trick you into feeling colorless. John H. Johnson used to say, "No matter how big you get, white people can find a way to remind you of the Negro you are." In other words, don't ever think you have so much money that you can't get fired, arrested, publicly humiliated—or all three. There was a time when black people were afraid to let their white bosses and coworkers know how they were spending their money, because someone might think that they were doing "too well." If they had nice cars and nice clothes, they opted to only be seen in them after working hours.

There was always the fear that the white people who signed their paychecks would find a way to take that money away from them. Most people I knew did everything they could to keep people from knowing how much or little they earned. I don't have that fear, although I'm not the kind of guy who spends money on a fleet of cars or a fleet of motorcycles. In fact, I don't have a fleet of anything, except maybe jogging suits.

Whether you want it to happen or not, once you start making lots of money the media begins publishing how much you're worth. Magazines like *Forbes, Fortune*, and *Black Enterprise* devote entire issues to lists of people's annual salaries. It's funny we never see a list of the one hundred wealthiest journalists highlighting the amounts of money they earn.

In 2004 when we announced the merger between our company, Reach Media, and Radio One I got outed for the first time. In the past when I'd signed contracts and deals, people had taken a stab at how much I was earning and how much I was worth but no one really knew for sure. But with the Reach Media–Radio One deal there it was in black and white. Tom Joyner sells 51 percent of Reach Media for $56 million. It felt weird to see that figure on paper and I felt like I had lost the financial anonymity I had enjoyed for so long in my career. One thing for certain was when people asked to borrow money from me there was no way for me to say "I ain't got it!" I could just picture broke people coming up to me with the article in their hand!

Does making $56 million change a brother? It didn't change me, but it changed the way people thought of me. Other people became more interested in what I was doing with my money and all of a sudden I became a different sort of role model than I had been in the past. There's a certain amount of responsibility that comes along with having lots of money, and the more public your money is, the bigger your responsibility is to spend it wisely.

I had made an offer before the deal went through to purchase Morris Brown University and its owners must have thought I was bluffing. Once the article came out, they called right away and were ready to talk again.

In reality, making $56 million didn't feel all that much different from making $10 million, as I had the year before. Sure it *was* more but I've grown to expect more each time I move to the next phase. I have been blessed to have made more money with each job I took beginning with my first radio job where I earned $90 a week. I've been in the business a long time and really have taken lots of baby steps over the years to get where I am now, and I think that's what kept me from going buck wild and trying to buy something like the entire state of Ohio.

That's another reason I can't harshly judge entertainers and athletes who suddenly become millionaires and get into trouble.

I once heard a troubled NFL rookie say that before he signed his multimillion-dollar contract not only had he never had a checking account but no one in his family had either. When you get a huge amount of money all of a sudden, there's no way to know what to do with it. Nothing can really prepare you for going from rags to riches.

The other good thing about earning more and more in relatively small increments over the years is that you're able to mature along with your money. At this point in my life quintupling my earnings from $10 million to $56 million didn't cause me to change. But back in the day when I went from earning $200 a week to $500 I nearly lost my mind! You couldn't tell me anything. If I did anything to offend you during that time (and I'm sure I did), please forgive me. I was drunk with semi, semi, semi wealth.

If you're like most black people and weren't born into money, once you find wealth, get some good advice from people you trust. Find people who have managed their money well and emulate them. I learned before it was too late to keep an eye on my money, and to always have a personal hand in how every penny is spent. It's time-consuming but it's worth it.

I'm really old school, especially when it comes to banking. I don't use ATMs and I want any money I acquire to be in check form, and to be placed in my hand, not wired to my account—I don't care whether it's $56 or $56 million. Don't think I didn't fill out my deposit slip for $56 million, take it to the bank teller, and, oh yeah, get $5 cash back for a little pocket money.

I've never discussed money one-on-one with Oprah, but in a sense, she's my financial role model. She's handled her fortune very wisely and I've emulated a lot of moves that she's made in the business world. When the *Oprah Winfrey Show* became nationally syndicated in the 1980s, King World owned her show. That company would sell it to markets and split a percentage with her—it got about 80 percent and she got the rest. After a few years, O flipped the script, bought the rights to her show, and started syndicating herself.

I did the same thing with the *Tom Joyner Morning Show* that was originally syndicated by ABC. After forming Reach Media, we began syndicating the *Morning Show* ourselves, and, like Oprah, bought our financial freedom. When you think about it I've emulated Oprah in life as well as in business. She hooked up with a pretty man, I hooked up with a pretty woman. She got in good shape by taking her chef and trainer everywhere she goes, and so do I. Don't get me wrong. I certainly don't have anywhere near Oprah's kind of money. She's so rich she's got money to throw away! What else would you call giving a brand-new Rolls-Royce to Stevie Wonder? He doesn't even drive!

But I'll tell you this, if I did have as much money as Oprah

I'd do one other thing she's done that no one knows about: I'd buy a better version of myself! Come on! There are two Oprahs, one who is fine and one who is superfine! That's what billions can do for you. I would think there were two Donald Trumps too, but check out that hair! No one would duplicate that on purpose. When I make enough money I'm going to buy another Tom Joyner. He'll be thin, have a full head of hair, and walk around happily with a piece of cake in one hand and cookie in the other!

I guess if I've learned one thing about acquiring wealth that I'd like to pass on, it would be *let money change you . . . for the better*. It can. You can use it for good, and the more you do, the more money you'll get, just like the church hymn says. Don't set out to make a lot of money. Set out to provide something that people want or need. The money will come.

For years, I had been looking for a way to save Historically Black Colleges and Universities and I couldn't imagine where I could get enough money to do it. When I got the $56 million I knew exactly how I wanted to spend it—giving black people places to learn skills that will allow them to achieve financial success in the real world.

Everybody won't get wealthy and I don't think everyone wants to be. I think what most people want is to be equipped to get a job that allows them to earn the money they need to provide themselves and their families with all the stuff they need and a lot of the stuff they want—good food, good health, and good relationships. Now that's rich.

chapter thirteen

"The Second Time Around"

. . . in a marriage, a grown man can't leave the house alone without a good reason . . . you have to be going out for something that your spouse agrees you need.

I NEVER was a good player. First of all I was fat, had nappy red hair, and absolutely no game at all. The fact that my great-grandfather was a stud slave, a man slave masters used only to breed with the female slaves, was irrelevant because none of what he had trickled down to me. I just watched every other guy I knew get to first, second, third bases, and even home plate with the fast girls in town. Meanwhile, for me, nothing. Maybe that explains my hatred for the game of base ball. All this time I've been blaming it on the fact that the game is boring. In reality, maybe it's just a stark reminder of my dismal love life as a Tuskegee teen.

As I got older, things weren't much better. When I entered Tuskegee Institute I was a kid just seventeen years old. I was one of the younger freshmen on campus, not because I was one of those supersmart kids who graduated early from high school. It was kind of the opposite of that. I was part of an experiment to find out what would happen if kids like me who hadn't proven to be high achievers academically were allowed to go to a four-year college without taking the normal steps. No SAT test, no placement test, no admission test, not even a spelling test. I was all for the program and before I knew it, I was in college, once again following in the huge footsteps of my brother who also attended Tuskegee.

Even though I was in a new environment with some new people from other parts of the country, my record for not scoring with the women remained pretty consistent. Finally, the woman who became my wife and mother of my sons showed an interest in me, and before we entered our senior year of college, we were married. So the second reason I was never a good player is because I barely got any practice. Dora and I were married for twenty-six years, and, when our marriage ended, I was back in the game again, just as green as I was the first time around.

When you marry young, you literally grow up with your spouse, or at least that's the idea. People say during our twenties we are trying to figure out who we really are and in our thirties we actually begin to figure it out. By the time we reach our forties (if we're lucky) we finally know who we are and what we want out of life. We also feel like it's our last chance to achieve it. Men, especially, start to get a "now or never" kind of mentality and it can cause us to make some life-altering decisions.

Although marriage no longer fit into my life at the time, marriage had been very good to me and for me. Without a partner by my side, I don't think I would have accomplished most of my professional achievements, and I certainly would not have had my sons. The statistics show that marriages between people as young as we were are less likely to survive, but Dora and I beat those odds.

Marriage isn't only a different world—it's a different planet. Things that are perfectly acceptable in marriage are completely alien to the single world; things like watching the exact same television shows in two separate rooms or yelling to each other about what you see on different channels. "You watching channel eight?!!! Turn to it quick! Your movie is on! Your favorite part is coming up!"

Another thing that goes without saying is that in a marriage, a grown man can't leave the house without a good reason. When you're single, you can just grab your keys and take off day or night. But when you're married, in order to get out of the house alone, you have to be going out for something that your spouse agrees you need.

Somewhere right now there's a married man, wondering when and how he'll be able to leave the house just for a little while. He may want nothing more than to clear his head but he can't go yet. He's got to wait until the family needs a quart of milk or something. A sneaky married man has probably, in an act of desperation, poured a perfectly good carton of milk down the drain just so he can leave the house alone. I don't condone that, but I can't blame him. A husband's inability to come and go as he pleases explains why a lot of men who get off work at five don't show up back home until eight. They've got to take freedom where they can get it!

Marriage takes you out of the cold, harsh world and puts you into a safe cocoon—a cocoon of un-hipness—but the sad part is, only single people know just how un-hip you are. It's not until you get back to the other world that you realize a whole lot of stuff was going on that you knew nothing about. Like comedian Earthquake says of marriage, it's like having regular TV when it seems like everybody else has cable.

When I entered singlehood, for the second time, I had all the trappings of a player. I had a good-paying job, a bachelorized home, and something I would later live to regret, a two-seater Mercedes that talked too much. If anything will bring the players in our society down it will be technology.

Maybe it was just my luck that I tried to become a player during one of the biggest technology booms this world has seen. Computers were taking over the two most important tools of a player's trade—the car and the telephone. From the time the telephone had been invented until the mid- to late-'80s the phone hadn't changed a darn bit. The only progress it had made was going from rotary to push button. Someone woke the phone scientists up around 1989. Then all hell broke loose and it's only gotten worse. Call waiting, caller ID, pagers, answering machines, cell phones, car phones, star 69, call block, e-mail, instant messaging, laptops, Palm Pilots, two-ways, Blackberries, On*Star, even TiVo can all be used for evil. There are just too many modes of communication for a player to succeed these days. And for an old-school country boy from Tuskegee, it was really more than I could contend with. I was already dealing with the changes in entertainment systems and that was a job in itself.

We all have a limit to how far we will let technology bring us. I've gone from 45s and albums to eight tracks, from reel-to-reels to cassettes and CDs. I got off the train at CDs. That's as far as I'm willing to go. No downloading music, no MP3s, no iPods. If I had my way, the fax machine would be as high-tech as I would ever get, but I was forced to have a very limited involvement with computers. I only recently got a cell phone because I need to check my messages on the road.

The last time I had been single, I lived in a place where everyone in town had the same phone prefix. If you wanted to reach someone by phone all you needed to remember were four digits. That was it. When I would overhear players using the line, "Let me get those seven digits," I had no idea what they were talking about.

I tried to be a player but it didn't take me long to realize I had simply been out of the game too long . . . or more to the point, I had never been in it in the first place. I was getting slammed at every turn. It was exhausting, and I think people may have been pointing and laughing at me behind my back. There was a lot of hate out there—even from my car.

My two-seater Mercedes had a phone system that talked back to you, in a female voice, of course. You could ask "her" if you had any phone messages and "she" would tell you who called. Once I had a female friend in the car with me and when I asked my car if anyone had called, that evil "woman" began to list about seventeen names that I'm willing to swear I'd never heard of. I don't know if my date had gotten together with the female computer or whether the computer was just hatin' on a brother; either way, I felt like an idiot trying to get "her" to shut up.

A talking car isn't the only thing that can bust a player. There are all kinds of other subtle ways that technology can mess up a player's evening. Computers keep records of everything you buy, everything you order, heck, probably everything you do, period. Something as simple as ordering a pizza can be disastrous. Even as inept as I was as a player, I knew not to let a date answer the phone, but using it to order a meal? What could go wrong? I'll tell you. She orders a pizza and as soon as your phone number comes up they have a record of who you are and what you ordered the last time you called. The pizza parlor clerk says, "I see that last night you ordered a large cheese pizza with mushrooms and black olives and two slices of cheesecake, one chocolate, one strawberry, would you like the same thing tonight?" Your date looks at you and says she wasn't at your house last night, why hadn't you mentioned that you had just had pizza the night before and why would you order strawberry cheesecake when you told her earlier you were allergic to strawberries? Even the most experienced players would be stung by something like this. Me? I pretended to pass out.

After a few years of being in the game, it became way too apparent to me that being a player is not for everyone. I didn't admit it to anyone but I knew I had to get out of the game. I met Donna Richardson after she was a guest on the *Tom Joyner Morning Show*. I wasn't looking for love but I was looking for a new trainer. It had been several years since my divorce. I had gained weight after my marriage ended and was having trouble focusing and staying committed to dropping the pounds. Donna started working with me and we discovered we had a lot in common. She was a very hard worker, dedicated to her profession, and extremely independent. And oh yeah, did I mention fine? She also enjoyed traveling and I was intrigued by the fact that she would up and go to all kinds of exotic places on her own. We became friends and fell in love. I was officially out of the players game and glad to be back where it was safe.

Some guys are just meant to be married and I think I'm one of them. I wasn't the kind of man who ran away or was coerced into getting married. I was happy to do it both times. When people ask me why my first marriage failed, I tell them it didn't. I don't think you can label something that lasted more than twenty years a failure. Failing and ending are two different things.

My parents were married for more than forty years. They weren't much different from any of my friends' parents in Tuskegee. I saw them as two strong people who each had a big role in raising my brother and me. As a couple, they were together but they weren't outwardly affectionate toward each other. Their love for each other was something we assumed but was never really talked about. They were a generation of people who, for the most part, married until death and they were less selfish than the generations that followed because they often put their commitment to family above their own personal happiness and dreams. My mama and daddy may have been having fun along the way, but they sure didn't look like it. One of the things I decided was that when I got married, fun would have to be a big part of it, and, if you know me at all, you know I have no problems with public displays of affection.

I didn't learn much about keeping a marriage happy from my parents but they did show me the benefits of being raised in a two-parent home and are probably the reason I wouldn't have had it any other way for my boys. Now that they're men they feel strongly about marriage, family, and children and the fun that comes with it. Kids gain stability, support, and equilibrium when they witness the two people they love most living, working, and loving together. It's not a foolproof formula for success in life, but it does stack the odds in their favor. In a perfect world, we would all move heaven and earth to keep our marriages together. In our world, the majority of black kids are raised in single-parent homes headed by their moms.

Just like I'm pretty clear on my strengths and weaknesses in my profession, I realize my strengths and weaknesses in my personal life too. That doesn't mean I don't make mistakes in both. Things can get you down but they don't ever have to keep you down. I've learned to do my best every day at work and at home—something I've gotten better at later in life. A great relationship is all about balance and achieving that balance is the trick. When you're young you don't know how much time it will take to attain your professional achievements, and sometimes you have your eye so focused on the prize ahead you don't notice a lot of the other things around you. Later in life most of us realize that personal achievements are as important as professional ones, and these take just as much dedication and perseverance.

I don't know if love is better the second time around or if it's just that you get another chance; every chance is an opportunity to do better and I'm all for that. I do know being married has taught me plenty. Being a player the second time, however, was worse!

chapter fourteen

"She's a Bad Mamma Jamma"

A man's long-range plans are different from a woman's. To a woman, long-range plans mean marriage. To a man, it's a three-day weekend.

QUESTION: HOW many single moms does it take to screw in a lightbulb, wash a load of clothes, help Ray Ray with his homework, braid Tasha's hair, bake a chicken, and iron her clothes for work? Answer: one.

When comedian Myra J. walks onstage after I introduce her as the poster child for single moms, hundreds of women, children, and men jump to their feet to cheer her on. I don't know when, if ever, single moms have been recognized in a positive way or whether they've ever had a champion they could relate to. I'd never even thought about it until we began to break down the demographics of our radio audience. And there it was. Something I can never allow myself to forget, forsake, or ignore—single mothers rule the world, or our world at least.

The majority of black children in the United States are raised in single-parent homes and most of those homes are headed by women. Whether the children of these woman have dads in their lives or not, mama is runnin' it.

We can talk all day about the virtues of two-parent homes, but, in reality, single mothers are and always have been doing the jobs of two people. Sometimes it's their choice, sometimes it isn't. It doesn't always matter how you got where you are. What matters is what are you going to do now that you're there. When you're a parent, no matter what label you have, if your children are your priority, you're on the right track and your kids will be too.

Keep in mind that I talk to members of our audience on a daily basis and see them in person a few times a month. I wouldn't call myself an expert on single moms, but I am an astute observer. I can't give the kind of advice Myra J. gives each week, but I can speak about a few issues from a man's perspective.

First, *stop* calling your baby-"daddy" your baby-"daddy" unless the other name you have for him is "that dirty low-down dog." "My child's father" is a lot more dignified and makes you sound less like a Ricki Lake guest! (You go, girl!)

Next, stop dwelling on the past. A lot of time and energy is being spent on the man who fathered your son or daughter and that time and energy could be better spent somewhere else. I have to believe he was okay to you at some point or why else would he have had the opportunity to father your children in the first place? If he's a bad guy who isn't supporting his family financially, take him to court and move on. If he's with someone else, you can't make him come back to you or, I should say, you can't make him permanently leave his other situation. If he's coming back every once in a while and you're letting him, you need to stop. Even if you don't mind that arrangement, it's not good for your children and it's confusing to the rest of us. One day you're cussing him out and the next day he's "your boo." You gain respect by earning it and if a guy can go from woman to woman to woman with no consequences he will. Don't make it so easy for him.

Whatever you do, don't bad-mouth your children's father in front of your children. The only thing it accomplishes is making them feel hurt or angry about a situation they didn't ask for and can't change. If you're doing it to try to keep them from having high expectations of their father, find a better way to do it. If he's not showing up or supporting them financially, explain that he's got some challenges and he would help out or spend more time with them if he could.

If you aren't sure who the father of your child is, don't go on a television show to find out. Use the process of elimination. When you narrow it down to two, ask your grandmother. She might not be able to tell you which one is the father but she can tell you which one isn't. Then get a DNA test to be sure. DNA tests are a sure thing, but before they were around grandmas were just as accurate at saying, "Now you know good and well that baby don't look nothing like that man!"

There seems to be more available women than men out there. This is bad news for women but good news for dating services. The Internet, newspapers, radio stations, game shows, and reality shows are all in the business of hooking people up. They're taking fate, chance, and "wait on the Lord" out of the equation and turning love into a very lucrative business. But if you don't have the time, the money, or the nerve to try to use the computer at work to find a man, you've got to use other measures. You might need to go the old-school route of trying to find your soulmate at one of the big "Cs": the church, the club, or the car wash. Unlike what you may have been led to believe by the '70s hit movie *Car Wash,* it isn't a great place to work, but it's a single mom's substitute for speed dating. Like speed dating, hanging out at a car wash allows you to find out a lot about a person in a short period of time. Unlike speed dating, it's free—except for the price of the car wash. If you meet a guy at the car wash, you know he has a car and you can learn a whole lot about a man from his ride, like his income, his marital status, whether he has children, and if he's a player.

There are some red flags, though. If he's driving a minivan, a station wagon, or an SUV without expensive rims that include any of the following: a child safety seat, disposable diapers, or the words "Just Married" written across the back window—move on. If a man has all of that and he still tries to approach you, then he's a player—and not a very smart one I might add.

Single moms need to be smart too. Sometimes all of the signs and signals are there that a guy is married and you either don't see them or you act like you don't see them. If you're at the point of asking other people whether they think the man you're seeing is married, he probably is.

A club is still a very common place for single moms to meet men but clubs are deceiving. You have on your best stuff and he has on his best stuff. He's on his best behavior and so are you. You both could be a little tipsy and on top of that it's dark. If you enjoy going to clubs and you know there's a chance that you might meet a guy you like, then go and have a good time. If you meet someone, that's icing on the cake. But if you're going to the club with the single mission of finding a man, the odds are not in your favor. Chances are you and every other single woman in the place have your eyes on the same three single men.

One excellent thing about clubs that makes it easier for everyone are line dances like the Electric Slide. Thanks to line dances a woman doesn't have to wait to be asked to dance anymore. She can just jump up there and do her thing. Wallflowers are a thing of the past. The only problem with line dancing is there's no longer anyone left at the table to watch the purses.

Church isn't necessarily the place for a single mom to find a mate, but single moms do and should go to church. The one thing single moms need most is a place where they and their children can find love and support, and many find these things at their places of worship. Many of the things you think only a man or a husband can fulfill in your life can be fulfilled by spiritual renewal, faith, and trust. Single moms need to love and respect themselves and know they are worthy of something more than many are willing to settle for. They should look for positive role models for themselves and strong male figures for their children if there's no man around for them to look up to. Boys and girls need to know there are good black men in the world who work every day, have respect for women, and take care of their children.

Single moms, your pastor may be a great man. He may look nice, speak well, have a nice home, and appear to be everything you want in the husband you may be seeking. But don't make the mistake of thinking he's perfect. He isn't. If you don't believe me, ask his wife, or better yet, watch her body language when he's preaching. A lot of women want the pastor to be the father or husband they don't have and they hold him up so high there's no way he can live up to their fantasies. They become disillusioned and move on to another church looking for the same thing from another imperfect man.

If you join a church for the right reasons you'll not only get a chance for spiritual fulfillment, but you will also—if you become involved in church activities—have something to do most evenings, and less time to dwell on negative things. Wednesday night Bible study, Thursday night choir rehearsal, Friday night singles club meeting, Saturday morning youth choir rehearsal, Saturday night for gossiping with church members on the phone—your slate will be full! If for some reason you don't want to be a part of the church or you aren't finding the kinds of role models you need there, then watch reruns of *The Cosby Show.*

A huge part of dating while being a single mom is the obvious—your children. Whether you meet a man in a club, at the car wash, at church, or at a drive-thru line at Popeye's, you have to make sure he's someone who is safe to be around your children. Remember, your children's well-being ALWAYS comes first. A new man in your life shouldn't become a part of your children's life unless the two of you have long-range plans. I'll repeat that. Unless the *two* of you have long-range plans. A man's long-range plans are different from a woman's. To a woman, long-range plans mean marriage. To a man, it's a three-day weekend.

Depending upon the age of your children you might bring different challenges to the world of dating from a man's point of view. Some single moms start dating while they have little babies. This poses all kinds of concerns for guys. If you have an infant, you either just got out of a relationship or are still, on some level, in a relationship with the baby's father. That means the new guy doesn't really know where he stands with you. I would suggest you wait until your kids are at least two before you start dating again. But if you can't follow that rule, how about this: Don't date if you're still breast-feeding.

If your children are school-age they sometimes are looking for a father themselves, so you should be extra careful not to get their hopes up every time you start to date someone you think has potential. Once your child does meet Mr. Could Be Mr. Right, introduce him as Mr. Blank, not as an uncle. And I don't care how long you're dating, don't have your child calling any man who isn't "Daddy." And don't start putting your date on daddy duty either. It's not cool for a man to go to your child's fourth-grade play and you shouldn't insist that he go.

Don't ask the dude you're dating to discipline your children either. You need to do it first so he won't even get the chance. One of your children is going to say to him soon enough, "You Not My Daddy!" Why rush the moment? Plus if your man yells at your kids, your kids are going to tell their dad, their granddad, their uncle, or someone who was just waiting for this other guy to get out of line. Next thing you know your family is on an episode of *Cops.*

Teenagers and grown children are easier for a man dating a single mom to deal with. They've usually got their own stuff going on and are happy that their mom has a distraction. However, these older children can be very protective of their moms, especially the sons. Sometimes just their presence lets the single mom's date know that he should come correct every time.

Another thing older children do for a guy is give him a gauge of just how old this single mom really is. If she claims to be thirty-five and so is her son—something's wrong.

Grandmothers are getting younger and younger these days and finer and finer. But still, every guy is not ready to deal with your children and your grandchildren. Pace yourself before springing the entire family on him and never force him to attend a family reunion. Not only will he discover how crazy your family members are, but he'll also be checking out your mother and your aunts to see how you're going to look in a few years.

Stop dating a man in prison, which is really a strange notion. How can you date a man who is in prison? Not only can't he take you out on a date, he can't do anything that you should be able to expect a man to do. If you were already involved with a guy who ended up going to prison, you may feel some obligation to maintain your relationship. I don't think it's a good idea but I can understand it. But if you meet a guy while he's in prison and start a relationship with him, I cannot cosign that move at all. The money you spend on telephone bills can better be used to send your kids to college.

I know the dating prospects for single moms sometimes seem bleak, but by looking at things from the male perspective at least you might be able to make some better decisions. Then, as if dating wasn't stressful enough for women with children, something else has been thrown into the mix. Single moms in the dating world now have to watch out for the Down Low Brothers. Back in the day, you knew when a guy was gay. Now, come to find out any guy can be gay—he can be single, he can be married, he can have kids, he can be the biggest player in town. This is just one more thing single moms don't need. These Down Low Brothers are tricky and apparently they don't think they're doing anything wrong. So single moms have got to go deep into their business and their past before they let these guys get close to them. I don't care how Down Low a brother is, there's something that should give you some kind of hint. A man should have a night or maybe two that he hangs out with the fellas, but if he claims he's going to poker night, bowling night, and gladiator night with his boys, you need to get suspicious.

There's no foolproof formula for raising healthy, happy, successful kids in a single-parent home, or a two-parent home either, for that matter. All any parent can do is their best. If you don't know what to do, look at what's worked for other people in your position. If the community you live in isn't able to offer you and your kids decent housing and schools, move. I know it isn't as simple as it sounds but it is worth the struggle in the long run.

My friend and "Turntable Brother" radio personality, Doug Banks, is one of the most successful deejays in the business. He was raised by a single mom in Detroit. She moved to a school district where there was a school with a radio curriculum with a real radio station. Doug was one of several kids from that program who moved into commercial radio and has had a remarkable radio career because of one decision his mom made. His mom did her job. She put his needs first. If you make a big sacrifice for your kids, single moms, it will pay off in the end. And it's the end that counts. Think about it. You might miss a few good times by devoting that extra attention to your children, or by investing in their future when you ensure that they learn a trade or attend college. But if you don't pay now you'll pay later. When those kids grow up they will either be your pride and joy or the cause of your pain and suffering. If they grow up to be strong, educated, and independent you'll have plenty of time to enjoy life and have all the fun you may have missed.

Someone once asked me whether I thought the attention I give to single moms glorifies unwed motherhood. See, that's the problem with conservatives. They've got it ass backward. They don't like to deal in reality. They think if you pretend something doesn't exist, it will disappear. I acknowledge single moms not to glorify the idea of unwed mothers but to give deserved support to all women. I'm just a deejay but I believe moms have the most important roles in the world. If you're a single mom the future is in your hands. Handle your business.

chapter fifteen

Cruisin'
(Spending a Week on the High Seas with 3,000 Black People with Credit Cards)

Of course, if you spend money on a vacation and return to no lights, no gas, and no water, you're going to have a lot of explaining to do. And absolutely no one will be interested in trying to look at your pictures in the dark.

TOM JOYNER, you know what happened the last time someone convinced a whole bunch of black people to get on a boat? We became slaves!" If you only knew how many people have said that to me since we began our annual Fantastic Voyage Cruise.

I have to admit, even though I never doubted that the cruise would be a successful venture, I did wonder if things like a bad economy and the aftermath of 9/11 would keep a lot of people from sailing with us. But black people are very resilient, and more than that, we're used to hard times.

When white people are complaining about a slow economy, layoffs, and the high cost of living, most black people are saying, "What else is new?" You know the old joke about how much do black people spend annually? The answer is: all of it. It's true we don't save as much as we should. Historically we've lived day to day, week to week, check to check. When we want to do something, we do it. When we want to buy something, we buy it. The real answer to the question how much money do black people spend is actually about $600 billion annually.

The first thing the success of the Fantastic Voyage Cruise taught me was that there's a whole industry out there with no interest in going after the money we black people have. Cruise lines, airlines, and tourism industries, with the exception of very few, are willing to settle for whatever African American business just happens to come their way. I'm just a deejay, but that's crazy to me. It's like two people selling pies on different corners. If one baker notices that the other guy has a line of people around the block he would be a fool not to try to offer something that would bring some of those people to his corner.

Back in the '90s, two things proved to me that black people had disposable income and were willing to travel outside of their city and even the country to see their favorite music groups: the Sinbad Soul Music Fest and the Essence Music Festival. Comedian Sinbad found great old-school acts and put on annual concerts over Memorial Day weekend in the Caribbean. The Essence Festival, a three-day event on Fourth of July weekend in New Orleans, brings thousands of black people from all over the country to see new and old-school acts and brings millions of dollars to the city of New Orleans every year.

Anyone who is close to me knows how bad and how long I wanted to do a Caribbean cruise with black folks. So, every once in a while I'll hear people say, "Tom, you talked to me about that cruise when it still was just an idea in your head. You didn't know how or when you were going to make it happen but you knew that you would." They all want to believe they were the first ones to hear about the cruise and I don't want to burst any of their bubbles.

My favorite thing about the cruise, other than the fact that it is the number one fund-raiser for the Tom Joyner Foundation, generating more than $1 million each year, is that it is proof positive that given the right opportunities black folks can and will rise to the occasion. There are three thousand black people from every socioeconomic category represented and they're all there to party—and the best thing is, they're partying like they're broke. There's no better party than a party full of broke people. Broke people are loud, broke people are wild, and broke people party like they just don't care. When you're wearing expensive clothes in an expensive house you have to care. If you spill a drink on someone's brand-new hardwood floors, you better care! But the cruise for some reason disarms the passengers just enough so that no one is trying to put on airs. People with money are dancing and sweating at 3 a.m. like they did when they didn't know how they were going to make their next rent payment. And people who really don't know how they're going to make their rent payment are sweating and dancing right next to them.

Professors, economists, sociologists, and politicians spend a lot of time and money trying to figure out the state of black America. If they came on board the cruise, they'd have their answer in seven days. My favorite kinds of lessons are the kinds that I don't have to study for and I've learned a lot of them in the years I've been cruising with black America.

Forget what you've heard about our saving patterns. We can save thousands of dollars to do something we really want to do. This is not the kind of advice you would get from a financial adviser but sometimes you need to forget about your debt and just take care of yourself. You only live once and those bills aren't going anywhere. They'll be there when you get back. As much as I'm for families taking trips together, sometimes you just have to do something for yourself without the kids, and maybe without your spouse. It can work wonders. When you're on a plane, one of the first instructions the flight attendant gives you is in the event that the air pressure drops, put on your own oxygen mask *before* helping the person seated next to you. You can't take care of other people until you take care of yourself. Of course, if you spend money on a vacation and return to no lights, no gas, and no water, you're going to have a lot of explaining to do. And absolutely no one will be interested in trying to look at your pictures in the dark.

The cruise has taught me that we really do like to help each other. An incredible amount of networking takes place on the cruise and the majority of it is legit. No matter what profession you're interested in there will be someone there with that job on the cruise, and if you talk to enough people, you'll come up with some new ideas of your own. But keep in mind that thanks to computer technology anyone can print up professional-looking business cards. Whether you're on land or sea, you need to beware of people like this. Some are pretty slick but others are easy to spot. If a man claiming to be a doctor gives you his card and the word "physician" is spelled with an "f," toss it overboard.

The people who come on the cruise have achieved a certain level of success. Either they've earned enough money for a cabin or they've convinced someone else to buy them one—either way takes some talent. And for the fellas who do bring a woman with them the cruise is in no way a guarantee of seven days and nights of romance. The same excuses women use at home can be used on a ship. What's worse, there's a chance that once on board the ship you'll hardly ever see her. Something is going on nonstop and I've seen many a man wandering around the boat looking for his $2,000 date. The words to that old song "Money Can't Buy Me Love" have never been truer.

Couples who go on the cruise should probably have an understanding up front. There won't be too many other opportunities to be around that many gorgeous people, male and female, and even the saintliest of people will find their eyes roving a bit. Trusting couples should just enjoy themselves with the "look but don't touch" clause in effect. If you have a spouse you cannot trust at home, heaven help you on the cruise. If, during your networking time, you run into a good lawyer—keep that card.

I don't actually know of any marriages that have broken up as a result of the cruise. But there have been a few weddings and a whole lot of babies conceived. This is a warning to people who are trying to get pregnant as well as to people who aren't. If you are not trying to get pregnant and you want to be safe, as you always should, the only thing I can say is BYO— bring your own. Courvoisier and condoms are big sellers and when the two are mixed—well you can imagine! The very last thing you want to buy on the streets of a Caribbean island are contraceptives, although if you're looking for them, in the words of my Jamaican brothers, it's "no problem, mon."

Black women travel in packs. The most popular cabins sleep four and most of these are purchased by sistas. Friends, cousins, classmates, sorors, sisters, any combination you can name, and they make it work. Normally, if you put more than two grown women in a house together problems begin to arise after about day three. The key to being on the cruise together is that there's very little reason to ever be inside the cabin. So the key to keeping women from getting on each other's nerves too much is to keep them away from each other enough so that when they do meet up they're happy to see each other. I've heard of four women who had a harmonious time on the cruise and fell out with each other on the cab ride to the airport.

Players who bunk four in a room have figured it out too. Not only is it cheaper but it's a good way for a guy to get into a woman's cabin by explaining that there are too many brothers in his room. Here's a little tip for women: If you see four male roommates wearing matching sarongs, they may not be looking for female company.

Black women in particular have various reasons for not wanting to get into the water but they like to look water-ready. They're around the pool and on the beach in one-pieces, bikinis, wraps, sarongs, and thongs. Some of them just don't swim, but I think most of them don't want to mess up their hairdos. Never, whether you're on a cruise or not, throw, pull, or push a black woman into a body of water. Not unless you're heavily insured.

Another thing the cruise taught me about black women is that they are really okay with their bodies. Every body type and size is on board from zero to forty. Society may try to tell women fine is fourteen or below but the sisters are not hearing that at all. If age ain't nothin' but a number, neither is size. On the beach, at the pajama party, the concerts, in a toga!—you name it, the big girls were representing and there was no shame in their game. Work it, ladies!

I don't think you can board the cruise ship without at least one camera and even though I try every year to load the cruise up with people-friendly celebrities, I've learned that a lot of celebrities have issues. They love their fans while they're on-stage but when it comes to one-on-one contact, a lot of performers can't handle it. They get testy, they get paranoid, and some of them get downright evil. That's something I will never get. How are you going to be a celebrity and not feel comfortable with the people who made you what you are?

Stars may be able to get away with blending into the crowd with some people but not black people. Black folks expect their celebrities to be the way we think they are 24/7. If you're a singer or an actress who appears to love all her fans like a sister, you better be just like that when you come off of the stage. They'll treat you like a celebrity when you act like a real person, but if you go diva on them (male or female) black people are going to let you know about yourself. They want pictures and they want autographs and in my opinion they should be obliged. I do think fans should honor the meal and bathroom rules. If a celebrity is sitting down having a meal, it's only fair to allow them to finish eating before you approach them for pictures . . . if nothing else so they can make sure they don't have crumbs on their face and food in their teeth. And if you see a celebrity approaching the bathroom I think it goes without saying that you should let them take care of their business. Never follow them inside and if you happen to be inside while they're in a stall, come on! I can't speak for females but it's no way for a guy to sign an autograph while relieving himself, and if he does, you shouldn't want that pen or paper back!

Maybe the bigger you become, the easier it is to lose touch with "the people," but when they're right in your face it seems to me you have only one choice and that's to show them a little gratitude, whether you feel like it or not. I'm just a deejay, but if you see me out in public, please stop me and say hello. If you don't, my feelings will be hurt. Throw in a hug too. I'm needy, I admit it.

People just want to have a good time, and when you show them a good time and give them value and more for the money they've spent, they show you nothing but love. To answer Rodney King's monumental question "Why can't we all just get along?" I believe the answer is "We can." There's something about letting black people know we are trusted and expected to act right that results in a problem-free event. It's police and security guards milling around, looking at you, and telling you to back up, that bring out the worst in us. There was a time when we lived in communities together, watched out for each other, and didn't even lock our doors. The cruise reminds me of that time.

Even though the cruise is primarily promoted to a black audience, a lot of white passengers join us each year and they get in where they fit in. Hey, until the Fantastic Voyage Cruise whenever we cruised, black people were in the minority and we had to do the best we could. We went to the disco and had to wait to hear a song we wanted to dance to and we even had to forsake spades for shuffleboard. The cruise brings white people into a world most of them have never seen, and by the end of the seven days, they've gotten their hair cornrowed and are downloading the Gap Band's greatest hits. If it was a little overwhelming to them at first, well, they've gotten an insight to how we feel most of the time.

If you're really interested in studying what makes the Fantastic Voyage Cruise work, I'll tell you. The majority of first-time cruisers join us because we were the first to invite them. If you reach out to black people with your advertising dollars, your promotional dollars, and philanthropy, we'll thank you with product loyalty. It's not rocket science. It's common sense. Black media traditionally have been treated like second-class citizens and it will continue until we demand better. Black newspapers and magazines, black radio and TV, have to beg for ad dollars despite the billions we spend on the very products the advertisers are selling. We ought to be discerning consumers and only spend the money with people who prove they want our business. If advertisers can't invite us to buy what they're selling, we ought to cruise on by.

chapter sixteen

"Fight the Power"

Fighting the power is good,
but becoming the power is
even better.

ONCE WHEN I was a student at Tuskegee, and performing with the Commodores, the guys and I had just returned from the road when we heard that some students had a bunch of the school's trustees and administrators locked in one of the administration buildings on campus. This took place during the annual board of trustees meeting and the board was made up of some of the country's richest people including members of the Rockefeller and Carnegie families, who along with other trustees made huge donations to black colleges. These donations were made partly out of altruism and partly because black colleges ensured the separation of the races.

One of the biggest fears some white people had was not so much that integration would lead to black people getting a "white" education, but that the mixture of the races would lead to interracial dating. If they could have looked into a crystal ball to see how many black NBA players have white wives and girlfriends they probably would have dropped dead.

Since I had just breezed into town I wasn't involved at all in the seizing of the trustees but I was aware of some of the issues that were on the table, mainly because my brother, Albert, as student body officer, was one of the negotiators. We wanted curfews lifted from the girl's dorm. We wanted an end to mandatory ROTC, and, the issue nearest and dearest to my heart, we wanted to be entitled to "make up" the meals we missed in the cafeteria. As it stood, if you missed breakfast, (which I missed a lot because I stayed up late and slept late), you were just out of luck. In my mind, if I had missed out on twenty-five breakfasts I should be able to go into the cafeteria at any given time and get those twenty-five meals I missed all at once. I knew there was no way I could actually eat twenty-five stacks of pancakes, but I could get twenty-five cartons of chocolate milk and that was worth going against the system any day of the week!

I found a way to get into the building where all the commotion was taking place. The lock-in had actually been part protest and part party, so in a sense this was the original party with a purpose. My brother and his crew had eaten all of the food and drunk all the liquor that had been provided for the trustees. I missed out on that segment of the fun but I was there for something almost as good—the cameras. People were taking pictures and I tried to be in as many shots as I could.

By this time Sheriff Lucius Amerson, the first black sheriff in the county, threatened to bring in the National Guard, and before I knew it the armed Alabama National Guardsmen began pulling up on campus in tanks. I don't think any of us realized the danger that we were in. When the smoke cleared, no one had been hurt, we got most of the concessions we'd wanted, and oh yeah—I was suspended from school. Even though I swore to anyone who'd listen that I had nothing to do with locking the trustees in the building, I was identified in several photographs. Later, when I returned to school I enjoyed my twenty-five cartons of chocolate milk while they lasted, which wasn't very long. Allowing students to get extra meals all at once almost broke the school. Still, it taught us that if we were passionate about something, took a stand, and were willing to make a sacrifice, we could force a change. We took on the most powerful people in our world at the time and not only did we not blink, some of us were crazy enough to smile for the camera.

Growing up when and where I did, I couldn't help but believe I had a right and a duty to go up against anything I felt was wrong. Once I got into radio, I used the airwaves as a soapbox to protest on more than one occasion. I may not be the most talented, the most articulate, or the most polished person in the world, but I do have a big microphone and I'm not afraid to use it!

WHEN I was a local deejay at KKDA-AM in Dallas I took on the Dallas Police Department with a bit I called "Drop a Dime on the Man." The department had gone crazy with radar detectors, especially in south and west Dallas, the two black sections of town. Cops were perching in trees, hiding in ditches, and behind camouflaged trucks. They were writing so many tickets they began to set up roadblocks so they could check names and license numbers for unpaid tickets. My listeners began complaining to me and I could hear the frustration and helplessness in their voices. The only thing I could think to do was to turn it back around on the policemen. I told my audience if they spotted a cop with a radar detector to call me and I'd report it on the air. When they would call I'd break from whatever I was doing, playing music, commercials, doing news—it didn't matter—cut in, and alert drivers to a reported radar trap.

I'd be lying if I said I got into radio so I could be a voice for the voiceless. Especially because I don't believe any of us really are voiceless. Some of us just need a forum for expressing ourselves and I will take credit for making that forum available to my audiences for the past thirty-five years. What I've also tried to do is help our audience develop the tools for helping themselves.

When people have problems they're told to write or call their congressman. It sounds simple but a lot of people have no idea where to call or write their representatives or even who they are for that matter. That kind of information plus how to find your polling place and which elections are coming up in your community are all available on BlackAmericaWeb.com.

Whenever we take our show on the road the audience receives voter registration forms and they can also register to vote on the Web site. That's as easy as we can make it. Getting people to fill out registration forms, and even physically getting them to the polls, is a way to increase the involvement of black people in the political system, but that can't be the only answer. For me, the answer is educating and informing people so that they will have not just the drive to participate but also an urgent desire to participate.

Our political and judicial systems obviously don't always work in your favor, but they work better than nothing at all. Some people see things going wrong and think they don't have what it takes to make a change. Everyone seems to be waiting for another Dr. King. Did anyone ever stop to wonder what would have happened if Dr. King had waited for a Dr. King? He was just a man with a vision and an urgent desire for change. As most people who played a role in the civil rights movement will tell you, in the beginning there weren't that many soldiers in the fight. It started, as most movements do, with a faithful few. And don't be fooled, some of them were trifling. You only read and hear about the ones who stayed strong, but a lot of people dropped out and a lot of people joined in the end when most of the hard work had been done.

The same thing probably happened with the Underground Railroad. You read about Harriet Tubman and the people who followed her to freedom, but you never read about the ones who said, "Y'all go on. We's fine." If you believe you're right you can't always wait for a group to back you up. Sometimes a drum major for change has to be a whole band. So, march on . . . even if you stand to lose something big . . . like your job.

After hearing about a list of companies who advertised in the mainstream media, but didn't advertise in media that targeted black people, we decided to challenge one of them. We just happened to choose computer and software retailer CompUSA. Our initial intentions were never to boycott or even bring public humiliation to the company. We simply wanted to meet with the head of the company to discuss how it might consider making plans to advertise with the sizable black consumer market.

For several days, Tavis Smiley appealed to CompUSA in his live commentaries aired on the *Tom Joyner Morning Show* twice weekly. For weeks we were ignored by the company. So the next step was to prove to CompUSA that black people not only bought computers but that a large number of them were buying them from its retail stores. We asked our audience members to send their CompUSA receipts to the company and they did. They also called the company and wrote letters. I almost hate to unleash our audience on companies because they will shut a switchboard down, so even though the top people at the company eventually get the message, it's the poor receptionist who has to suffer. In our zeal to get our point across, sometimes we don't wait for the receptionist to connect us to the right people. So I'm sure that for days all she was hearing was "How come you don't advertise to black people!?"

In the midst of all this the executives at CompUSA were getting annoyed and my then-distributor ABC Radio wasn't too pleased either. At one point I was even told not to even mention CompUSA until further notice. So, the very next day I started the show with the words "CompUSA, CompUSA, CompUSA, CompUSA." I had to do it. Not to prove that I couldn't be bossed but more to prove that I couldn't be bought. This was an issue that was important, not only to me, but to black media period. If I had to get fired for doing something right, fire away.

After ten weeks the president of CompUSA finally met with us. CompUSA eventually began to advertise in black media but not on our show, hired ad agencies specializing in marketing to African Americans, and even offered everyone who sent in receipts a 10 percent discount on CompUSA products. Did CompUSA finally get the message? Did we really win? Was the problem solved? The answer is probably no to all three questions.

The goal was never for CompUSA to advertise on the *Tom Joyner Morning Show*. It couldn't have, even if it had wanted to; we had no more advertising space to sell. The goal was to let advertisers know that it makes good business sense to use black media to reach black consumers. They can't continue to assume they'll get the African American consumer regardless of what they do. Or maybe they can assume that until black consumers stand up and say that's enough?

First of all, black people need to understand how doing nothing hurts us. What happens when CompUSA or any other company doesn't buy commercial time on your favorite radio station, or ads in your favorite magazine, or spots on your favorite television show? It's simple. Your favorite station, your favorite magazine, or your favorite television show will lose money and then it will disappear. That's what happened to the magazine *Heart and Soul,* it's what happened to *Living Single,* and it's what happened to the hundreds of black-owned newspapers that no longer exist. All media depend on advertising dollars to survive. Viewership and readership are important but only because they determine how much money an advertiser will spend. In theory, the more viewers a program has, or the more readers a publication has, the more advertising dollars it can charge. *Unless* it's a black program or publication; then, no matter how popular or good it is, advertisers expect to pay less to sponsor it than they would pay to a comparable—or even to an inferior—program or publication having a white audience.

In the end, it's the advertisers that keep us from seeing ourselves represented more on the airwaves and on the newsstands, and the only way to get their attention is with our wallets, and even that's no guarantee. When something is ONLY about money, fairness, honesty, and equality go out the window. The golden rule turns into "He with the most gold rules."

My passion toward getting companies to advertise with black media was never only about money. It was always about respect and commitment but mostly it was about righting a wrong that's gone on way too long—taking money from black America and never giving anything back.

I'm just a deejay and I can't right every wrong perpetuated on black America, but I can do the best I can with the resources I have. When Reach Media Inc. merged with Radio One, a black-owned, publicly held communications empire, together we could become a huge force in the media world. My goal for Reach Media from the beginning was for it to be an African American–owned media company that would be all things to black people. The merger with Radio One allows us to get further with our vision faster. Sometimes you can wait for a change to come but if it looks like it's not going to happen you have to make your own way. Fighting the power is good but becoming the power is even better.

chapter seventeen

Oh! Oh! Oh! What I've Learned from the Show!

Why doesn't the ATM give coins? Sometimes all you need is 15¢.

I F YOU can find a job where you are guaranteed to laugh out loud at least twenty times an hour, take it! And if you can learn something too, even better! Even though I make a living running my mouth, I've been doing some listening and observing over the years and I've made a lot of discoveries. Some may not be profound and they may even be downright silly. Like, I know I'm just a deejay and I don't even have any hair, but why are most black beauty shops closed on Mondays when they know your hair is jacked up after the weekend? And the better the weekend, the worse the hair! I can't believe sisters haven't risen up in protest!

Why is Bible study on Wednesday night and why can't it be changed when a black television show is depending on those black viewers for its survival? White people just don't understand that when they air a black show on Wednesday nights, it's the kiss of death. Or maybe they do know. Hmmm. Oh yeah, I'm big on conspiracy theories.

Why do we have to pay for more utilities than we need? Why can't we purchase electricity, deli style? For example, you only have $50 in the bank; shouldn't you be able to get $20 worth of lights, $17 worth of gas, and put whatever is left on water? It's our money, we should be able to spend it any way we want. And while we're on the subject of money, why doesn't the ATM give coins? Sometimes all you need is 15¢. You can put that down on a slice of bologna or if things were run my way . . . a slice of heat. Here are some other things I've learned:

Shout-outs are dumb.

The reason we don't do shout-outs is because, in most cases, a shout-out is only interesting to the person who is doing the shouting out and the person it's intended for. And let's face it, rather than giving a shout-out to your thirteen-year-old daughter who made the drill team, it's much more meaningful to just walk into her bedroom and say, "Hey, great job! Now stop shaking your behind and do your homework."

Be flexible.

We lifted the No Shout-Out rule on the show when the war on Iraq began because we realized that because our show can be heard all over the world and on the Armed Forces Network, it was a great opportunity for spouses, family members, friends, and, yes, skeezers to give shout-outs to the men and women who were serving in the military. It was moving to hear family members send messages to their loved ones. Many moms and dads really had no idea where their children were or what they were doing. All they knew is that they were "over there" fighting and they were ready for them to come home. And in consideration for the security of our country, it's a good thing some of those moms had limited information because what little they did know, they told! You can almost always count on mama and Big Mama to give out too much information. If you don't believe me, call up a friend's mom and ask where that friend is. Nine times out of ten, Mrs. Whoever will tell you where that friend is, when he's expected back . . . and she'll offer to give you his cell phone number!

Always respect the Queen.

There's just one Aretha Franklin. She is our Queen. And when I mention "Her Soulness," I'm talking about our one and only . . . no disrespect to Queen Latifah, Queen Elizabeth, the Queen of Hip-Hop, Mary J. Blige, or the Queen of Rock & Roll, Little Richard.

Go with the bit.

When something funny is going on, even if, no *especially* if, you're the butt of the joke, don't fight it. Laugh along or be quiet. Don't try to explain, don't try to defend, don't try to retaliate . . . go with it. If you don't, the bit will turn on you.

What happens on the ship stays on the ship.

That goes for any *Tom Joyner Morning Show* event including the Fantastic Voyage Cruise, the Sky Show, the Tom Joyner Family Reunion, etc. It just means you can act a fool and you won't have to hear about it on the radio . . . most likely. Our intentions are good, but as long as there are digital cameras, video cameras, cell phone cameras, and (no offense) women who can't keep secrets, then these photos, videotapes, and stories will leak more than a wet Jheri curl.

We can only hold a pose so long.

The *Tom Joyner Morning Show* crew never objects to being photographed. We just ask, no, we beg, that you LEARN TO OPERATE YOUR CAMERA before you ask us to pose, especially if you see us heading toward the bathroom. Three minutes is a very long time when your bladder is full! Practice at home. And don't ask us if it flashed because we will say it did whether it's true or not!

Root for the home team.

When rooting for a sports team, the rule is as follows: *We root for the home team that represents a city where we're heard*. For example, if the Miami Dolphins were playing a team from Wyoming, we'd be for the Dolphins. If both teams are from markets where we are heard, we root for the team who has the most black starters. If both teams have a lot of black starters, we root for the team with a black coach. If both teams have black coaches, we root for the team with the coach who attended a Historically Black College or University. If both coaches attended HBCUs we root for the darker-skinned coach. If they're both pretty dark, then we go to the nose. (Hey, I don't make the rules, I just enforce them!)

Fat trumps skinny.

If two people are walking down a narrow hall or aisle in opposite directions, *the larger person has the right-of-way*. The smaller person is to simply drop his head, take a step to the right, and allow the larger person to pass. So, if you are frequently given the go-ahead to pass, you know what that means.

Don't call the IRS.

No matter how tempting the offer. Sometimes you hear stories that the government has unclaimed money that it owes. They tell you to call an 800 number to see if you may be one of those people. It's an evil plot. After all, if anyone knows how to get in touch with you, it's the government. If they can contact you when you *owe* money, they can contact you when you're *owed* money. If they want you to have that money, they'll send it to you! Don't call that number!

Keep up with your cell phone.
Especially if you're a player. Never lay it down. If you're cheating, you're going to get caught, but it shouldn't be because you left your cell phone somewhere!

You're going to get busted.
The only question is when. With the technology that's out today: two-way pagers, e-mail, On*Star, it's only a matter of time. Face it, people were getting busted back when they had nothing but a rotary phone and a bus pass. I'm thinking of writing a poem dedicated to players called: "How Can Thou Get Busted, Let Me Count the Ways!"

Stop videotaping.
Let's face it, the only person who wants to see your wedding and the birth of your baby is you, and you were there. And the "personal videotaping" you're doing, if it ends up in the wrong hands (and it will), will cause you nothing but grief, embarrassment, and possibly jail time. So just stop it!

If you get busted making a videotape, make a hit gospel song.
It worked for R. Kelly.

If you think you might get arrested, fix your hair.
There was a time when your mug shot would be seen only by a select few. Now, there are Web sites dedicated to showing the world nothing but jacked-up police photos. You've seen them. Allen Iverson's, Glen Campbell's, Nick Nolte's, Wynonna Judd's, and the mother of all mug shots, James Brown's. Granted, unless you're a celebrity, your mug shot may not make the news or the Internet, but you never know. So, just to be safe, fix your hair before you leave the house, es-

pecially if you're planning to drive a black Escalade with tinted windows down the highway while smoking weed.

Don't fry chicken naked.
However, if you do, forget what I said earlier and videotape it!

Call me.
If you want to get in touch with me and other black people, pick up the phone and call us. It worked back in the day, it works now. If I'm not home, leave it on the machine ... that's right, I said machine! If you e-mail me I'll get it eventually, but if you need me now, to paraphrase the great '80s group Skyy, I'll give you my number and a dime so you can call me anytime!

Huh?
When your woman asks you if her behind looks too big, act like you don't hear her.

Stand next to a fat person.
If you want to look thinner.

Don't test a big word in public.
We encourage people to improve their vocabularies, but a national radio show with eight million listeners is not the place to test a new word. Work on it at home, try it out on a friend, practice saying it a few times, before you call our show. Believe me, we're waiting in the cut for you to mispronounce a big word.

Nothing's off-limits.
Not my yellowness, my baldness, or my celebrity impersonations, which all sound a lot like Bootsy Collins.

Move out of your old neighborhood.
But spend your money there.

It's not easy for a dance to catch on.
You think it was easy for Chubby Checker and the Twist . . . it wasn't.

You can date out of your race.
But don't complain about dirty looks.

Hold on.
If you do something wrong, wait it out, you *can* make a comeback. Or better yet, keep going like you never did anything wrong, like Eddie Murphy.

Not all stalkers are necessarily bad people.
A few have given them all a bad name. Some of them are just trying to keep up with you.

Don't get mad if white people offer you watermelon.
If you really want some, make them cut it up and put it in a bowl with tropical fruit.

Give ugly a chance.
Even Halle Berry, Vanessa Williams, and Vivica A. Fox couldn't get it right with pretty boys.

If you win the lotto, quit your job.

If you're gonna quit your job, don't give too much notice.
That only works for white people.

Tell your boss to kiss your ass if you win the big lottery.
But if you win the football pool, just keep your mouth shut.

Increase your odds of winning the lotto.
Change your name to one that doesn't have a lot of vowels,
move to a small town, and try to look seventy-five years old.

Act like you don't want it.
It becomes easier to get.

Don't shave your head until it's necessary.
A bald head is nothing to play with.

They don't wear a lot of African stuff in Africa.
Don't go over there in a Kinte suit.

Don't trust a black man who doesn't have a mustache.
Unless he's Nelson Mandela.

Only root for boxers who split their verbs.
This is why I could never get behind Lennox Lewis.